COOKING IN CLAY

Joanna White

BRISTOL PUBLISHING ENTERPRISES
San Leandro, California

A NITTY GRITTY® COOKBOOK

Printed in the United States of America.

ISBN 1-55867-118-8

Cover design: Frank Paredes
Cover photography: John Benson
Food stylist: Suzanne Carreiro
Illustrator: John Balkovek

CONTENTS

AN INTRODUCTION TO CLAY COOKING

A clay cooker is a single vessel that can serve as a vegetable steamer, stew pot, soup kettle, fish poacher, brick oven and roaster. Clay is a porous material which, when saturated with water and heated in an oven, provides slow evaporation of steam from the pores. This creates a moist, enclosed environment that results in increased flavor, very tender meats and healthier foods. Clay pots require less fat, use less liquid (which means less nutrient loss), require little tending and can even brown meats. Once you experience the advantages of a clay cooker you'll wonder how you ever lived without it.

ADVANTAGES OF USING CLAY COOKERS

- Food cooks with a minimum of liquid and no additional fat.
- Food browns in clay, even with the lid on.
- Because food cooks in a closed environment with limited liquids, more of the essential nutrients and vitamins are retained.
- Ridges on the bottom of clay cookers elevate the contents to help the steam encircle the food and assist in totally browning the meat.

- Food can be kept warm by leaving the lid on the cooker after removing it from the oven.
- As long as you don't overfill the cooker, your oven will remain clean.
- Clay cookers may be used in the microwave very successfully. It is best to use lower power settings.
- Because of their attractive appearance, clay cookers can go directly from oven to table.
- Meats cook especially well in clay cookers because they have a tendency to stay moist and juicy.

RULES FOR COOKING WITH CLAY

- Clay must be soaked in water for at least 15 minutes before using. Note: If part of the clay pot is *completely* glazed, do not presoak that part before using.
- The clay cooker is always placed in a cold oven, and then the temperature is set.
- If you wish to add liquid to a heated clay cooker, be sure to heat the liquid first.
- Never use a clay cooker over a burner or heating element. If you wish to make gravy from pot juices, transfer liquid to a saucepan, add a thickening agent

and heat until thickened to the desired consistency.

- Avoid using a clay cooker under a broiler. If you wish to have browner meat or crispier food, it is best to remove the cover for 5 to 15 minutes before removing the cooker from the oven.

- Do not allow the cooker to touch the sides of the oven.

- Always set a hot clay cooker on a trivet or pad on a cold surface when it first comes out of the oven to prevent breakage from sudden temperature changes.

- To keep food from sticking and for easier cleanup, line the bottom of the cooker with parchment paper or brown paper. Do not line the lid because you want the maximum steaming effect.

- For recipe conversion I recommend that the temperature be increased about 50 degrees and cooking time be increased slightly (usually 10 to 20 minutes). Most books recommend increasing the temperature by 100 degrees, but I found that this generally overcooked the food.

- To microwave in clay: Clay pots actually enhance microwaving. Just soak the cooker in the usual manner and follow the standard microwave timing. A general rule for meats is 5 minutes on HIGH and 15 minutes on LOW for each pound of meat used. Increase cooking time if many vegetables are added.

CARE AND CLEANING OF CLAY COOKWARE

- When you first use a clay cooker, soak the top and bottom in water for 30 minutes, and then scrub with a brush or nonmetallic scrubbing pad to remove any clay dust residue.

- Do not use scouring powders because they will clog the pores and make the pot useless. Salt can be used as an abrasive cleanser.

- For general washing, wait until the cooker cools, wash it in water with a very small amount of dishwashing liquid and rinse. Do not put the clay cooker in the dishwasher — sudden temperature changes may crack the pot and excessive soap will clog the pores.

- For thorough cleaning, allow the clay cooker to soak overnight in the sink with water that has about 1/4 cup baking soda added to it. Then wash, using a brush or nonmetallic scrubbing pad. Follow this treatment after cooking fish or foods with strong seasoning.

- After washing, dry thoroughly and store with the lid inverted upside down in the bottom, ideally with a towel between the layers. Avoid storing the cooker with the lid sealed because it may become moldy if not carefully dried.

- If the cooker should become moldy, make a paste with baking soda and water, cover the cooker with the paste and allow it to dry. When the paste is dry, rinse with water and dry well.

- If pores become clogged, boil the clay cooker for 30 minutes to remove debris.

CLAY COOKERS: STYLES AND SIZES

GLAZED AND UNGLAZED CLAY

unglazed: Unglazed clay bakeware can soak up a considerable amount of water. This is best for tenderizing meats because of the super steaming quality. Use this type of pot for tougher cuts of meat, stews, roasts, cooking poultry, poaching, steaming and microwaving.

glazed: Glazed clay bakeware has a glaze which usually only covers the bottom cooker for easier cleaning. Oval and rectangular bakers, pie plates and casseroles are useful for recipes that do not benefit from the super steaming quality, such as pasta dishes like lasagna, casseroles and baked goods. This type of cookware is ideal for use as serving pieces.

STYLES AVAILABLE

All-purpose cookers come in several sizes. Small sizes have capacities of about 2 to 5 pounds (in deep and shallow versions). Medium cookers have capacities of roughly 4 to 6 pounds. Large cookers hold up to 14 pounds, and you can even get a very large clay cooker that will hold a 17-pound turkey. Some brands determine size by liquid capacity (based on the quantity that can fill the bottom part of the clay cooker). A handy size if you only have one cooker is a 3- to 3½-quart capacity, or medium size.

Cooking containers include: covered casseroles, garlic roasters, vegetable roasters, oval bakers, rectangular bakers, rectangular bakers with handles, and hot pots. All of these items can be used to serve the food as well.

Storage containers include: canisters, garlic cellars, mushroom cellars, pencil holders, bread crocks, utensil jars, spice jars, herb jars, wine coolers, onion keepers, cutlery drainers, honey jars, vegetable crocks, celery jars and preserves jars.

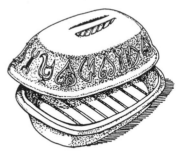

Other serving pieces are available, such as teapots, tea mugs, assorted pitchers, coffee mugs, assorted bowls, butter coolers and tankards.

SOUPS

MINESTRONE WITH PESTO

Minestrone is a hearty Italian soup traditionally made with beans, tomatoes and vegetables. Pesto adds real depth to this soup. Serve with a good, hearty bread and a tossed salad for a complete meal.

2 cups dried navy or pinto beans
water to cover beans
3 cans (14½ oz. each) beef broth
2 qt. water
2 tsp. salt
1 small cabbage, thinly sliced
4 carrots, sliced
1 can (1 lb.) tomatoes, slightly mashed
¼ cup olive oil
2 medium onions, chopped
2 small zucchini, chopped

2 stalks celery, sliced
1 fresh tomato, chopped
2 cloves garlic, minced
salt and pepper
1½ tsp. dried basil
1 tbs. tomato paste
¼ cup chopped fresh parsley
1 cup uncooked pasta (orzo, broken
  spaghetti or shells)
Pesto, follows

Cover beans with water and soak overnight. Discard water from beans and rinse beans thoroughly. Soak top and bottom of a large clay cooker in water for at least 15 minutes. Put beans, broth, 2 quarts water and salt in clay cooker, cover and place in a cold oven. Set temperature to 375° and cook for 2½ hours, stirring occasionally. Remove about ½ of the beans, mash in a blender and return to cooker with cabbage, carrots and canned tomatoes; cook 30 minutes longer. While mixture is cooking, heat oil in a skillet and sauté onions, zucchini, celery, fresh tomato, garlic, salt, pepper and basil until vegetables are tender. Add vegetables to clay cooker with tomato paste, parsley and pasta. Cook for 45 minutes. Taste and adjust seasoning. Serve in individual bowls topped with 1 tsp. *Pesto*.

PESTO

¼ cup butter, softened
¼ cup grated Parmesan cheese
½ cup chopped fresh parsley
¼ cup olive oil

1 tsp. dried basil
½ tsp. dried marjoram
¼ cup pine nuts
1-2 cloves garlic, minced

Blend butter with Parmesan until well mixed. Add remaining ingredients and process until mixed.

LENTIL SAUSAGE SOUP

Lentils are legumes that are very high in protein. Lentils come in various colors and vary slightly in flavor.

1½ cups dried lentils
3 cups beef stock
1 large onion, chopped
2-3 cloves garlic, minced
2 carrots, diced
2 stalks celery, diced
1 tbs. soy sauce

1 tsp. oyster sauce
½ lb. Polish kielbasa, or sausage of
  choice
1 tbs. vinegar
salt and pepper
minced fresh parsley or cilantro for
  garnish

Soak top and bottom of a medium clay cooker in water for at least 15 minutes. Combine lentils, beef stock, onion, garlic, carrots, celery, soy sauce and oyster sauce in clay cooker. Cover and place in a cold oven. Set temperature to 375° and cook for 2½ hours or until lentils are soft. Cut sausage into bite-sized pieces and add to cooker with vinegar, salt and pepper. Cook for an additional 30 minutes. Taste and adjust seasoning, sprinkle with parsley or cilantro and serve.

RED ONION AND BEET BORSCHT

Servings: 4-6

Red onions lend a slightly different flavor and really enhance the red color of this simple soup.

4 large red onions, peeled and thinly sliced
½ lb. beets, peeled and shredded
½ cup red wine vinegar, or balsamic vinegar
¼ cup butter
2½ tbs. flour
6 cups chicken broth
⅓ cup port wine, optional
sour cream for garnish

Soak top and bottom of a clay cooker in water for at least 15 minutes. Place onions, beets and vinegar in clay cooker, dot with butter and cover. Place in a cold oven, set temperature to 400° and cook for 1 hour. Remove from oven, stir in flour and add chicken broth. If desired, add port. Cover and cook for an additional 15 to 20 minutes or until mixture thickens. Taste and adjust seasoning. Serve each bowl of soup topped with a dollop of sour cream.

BASIL VEGETABLE SOUP

Basil is my all-time favorite herb — it really packs a flavorful wallop to vegetables.

1 can (15 oz.) white beans
3 carrots, pared and cut into rounds
3 small zucchini, cut into rounds
1 pkg (10 oz.) frozen cut green beans
3 cloves garlic, minced
salt and pepper
2 qt. beef or chicken broth
1 cup uncooked small pasta (vermicelli, shells, orzo, etc.)
½ cup tightly packed fresh basil leaves
grated Parmesan cheese for garnish

Soak top and bottom of a large clay cooker in water for at least 15 minutes. Combine beans, carrots, zucchini, green beans, garlic, salt, pepper and stock in clay cooker. Cover, place in a cold oven, set temperature to 400° and cook for 40 minutes. Add pasta and cook for an additional 20 minutes. Add basil and stir until basil is wilted. Taste and adjust seasoning. Serve with a sprinkling of grated Parmesan cheese.

BEEF VEGETABLE SOUP

This hearty soup makes a complete meal with the addition of a tossed salad, rolls and fruit cobbler for dessert. Browning the meat first enriches the flavor of the soup.

2 tbs. olive oil
2 lb. beef shank, cut into slices
1 medium onion, finely chopped
1 cup chopped celery
2 qt. water
2 cups tomato sauce
salt and pepper
1½ tsp. dried oregano

2 tbs. chopped fresh parsley
1½ cups sliced zucchini
1 cup frozen peas
1 cup uncooked thin spaghetti, broken
   into pieces
shredded cheddar or Monterey Jack
   cheese for garnish

Soak top and bottom of a clay cooker in water for at least 15 minutes. Meanwhile, heat oil in a skillet and brown beef on all sides. Combine beef, onion, celery, water, tomato sauce, salt, pepper, oregano and parsley in clay cooker. Cover, place in a cold oven and set temperature to 375°. Cook for 2½ to 3 hours or until meat is tender. Remove shank from cooker, cut meat from bones, discard bones and return meat to cooker. Add zucchini, peas and spaghetti. Cover and cook for an additional 15 to 20 minutes or until pasta is tender. Serve garnished with a sprinkling of cheese.

SPLIT PEA SOUP

Bacon and ham enhance this old standby. Garnishing with garlic croutons adds flavor as well as eye appeal.

4 slices bacon, diced
1½ onions, chopped
2 carrots, diced
2 stalks celery, diced
1 lb. dried split peas
1 smoked ham shank

1 bay leaf
¼ tsp. cayenne pepper
salt and pepper
3 qt. water
1 cup chopped ham
Garlic Croutons for garnish, follows

Soak top and bottom of a large clay cooker in water for at least 15 minutes. Put bacon in cooker, cover and place in a cold oven. Set temperature to 450° and cook until bacon is crisp, about 20 to 25 minutes. Remove from oven, drain off excess fat and add remaining ingredients, except chopped ham and croutons.

Re-cover, return to oven and reduce temperature to 375°. Cook for 2½ to 3 hours or until peas are tender. If you desire a creamy texture, remove ham shank and bay leaf, transfer soup to a food processor or blender and puree until smooth. Return soup to clay cooker, add chopped ham and taste, adjusting seasoning. Heat until ham is heated through. Serve with garlic croutons floating on top of soup.

GARLIC CROUTONS

6 slices dry bread
4 cloves garlic
1 cup vegetable oil
salt

    Cut bread into small cubes. Mash garlic. Heat oil in a skillet on a medium-low setting. Add mashed garlic and toss in bread cubes. Fry cubes, turning constantly, until golden. Drain on paper towels and sprinkle with a little salt. (The salt helps to reduce the oily taste.)

POTATO SOUP

Leeks add a subtle difference to this soup. Serve with a vegetable salad and rolls.

4 slices bacon or salt pork, diced
6 leeks
3 large boiling potatoes, peeled and
  sliced

1 qt. chicken stock
2 tbs. chopped fresh parsley
salt and pepper
1 cup sour cream

Soak top and bottom of a clay cooker in water for at least 15 minutes. Put diced bacon or salt pork in cooker, cover and place in a cold oven. Set temperature to 450° and cook for 15 to 20 minutes or until bacon is just barely beginning to brown. While bacon is cooking, prepare leeks: trim off root end and cut off top ⅔ of tough green leaves. Slice leeks in half and thoroughly wash between layers to remove grit. Cut leeks into thin slices and add to clay cooker with bacon, stirring gently. Reduce temperature to 400°, return covered cooker to oven and cook for 30 minutes. Add potatoes, chicken stock, parsley, salt and pepper and continue cooking for an additional 1 hour or until potatoes are tender. Puree mixture in a food processor or blender until smooth. Add sour cream and reheat if necessary (do not boil). Taste and adjust seasoning. Serve hot.

RICE AND HAM SOUP

This recipe can be varied by using pork sausage or chicken chunks in place of the ham. You can even substitute clams.

1 cup uncooked rice
1 clove garlic
2 tbs. butter
¼ cup olive oil
2 tbs. minced onion
3 tbs. tomato sauce
1 lb. smoked ham, cubed
2½ cups water
salt and pepper

Soak top and bottom of a medium clay cooker in water for at least 15 minutes. Combine rice, garlic, butter and oil in cooker, cover and place in a cold oven. Set oven to 400° and cook for 20 to 30 minutes or until rice is golden brown. Add onion, tomato sauce, ham, water, salt and pepper. Return to oven for an additional 45 minutes. Taste and adjust seasoning.

BOUILLABAISSE

Don't be put off by the list of ingredients. It is really a quick soup to fix that is definitely a meal in itself. Serve with a crusty French bread.

2 tbs. olive oil
1 large leek, washed, trimmed and thinly sliced
5 cloves garlic, minced
2 medium onions, chopped
1 can (28 oz.) chopped tomatoes
½ cup chopped fresh parsley
2 tsp. sugar
1 qt. fish stock or chicken stock
¾ cup white wine
grated peel of 1 orange
½ cup chopped celery
pinch cayenne pepper
pinch saffron
2 bay leaves
1 tsp. dried basil

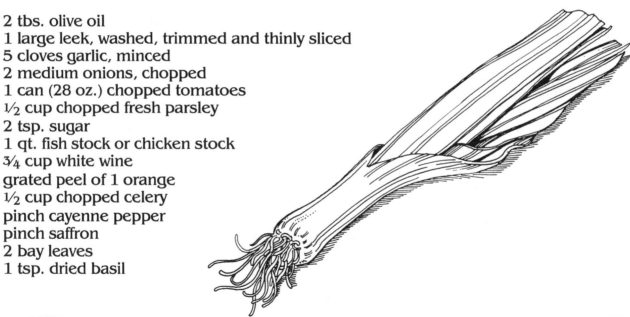

1 tsp. dried thyme
1 tsp. salt
pepper
1 lb. red snapper, cut into chunks
1 lb. scallops
½ lb. shrimp or prawns
½ lb. clams, shelled
½ lb. crabmeat, optional

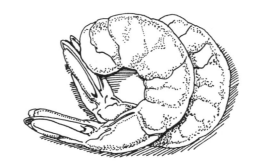

Soak top and bottom of a large clay cooker in water for at least 15 minutes. Combine oil, leek, garlic and onions in clay cooker, cover and place in a cold oven. Set temperature to 400° and cook until leeks are softened, about 30 to 40 minutes. Add remaining ingredients except seafood, cover and return to oven. Cook for an additional 45 minutes. Add snapper and cook for an additional 10 minutes. Add remaining fish and heat just until fish is warmed. Taste, adjust seasoning and serve immediately.

PUMPKIN BISQUE

A perfect soup for fall and winter. If you want to impress people, serve this soup in a hollowed-out pumpkin shell.

1/4 cup butter, melted
1 large onion, chopped
1 leek, white part only, chopped
1 can (16 oz.) pumpkin
4 cups chicken broth
1 tsp. salt
1 tsp. curry powder, or to taste

1/2 tsp. nutmeg
1/2 tsp. white pepper
1/2 tsp. ground ginger
1 bay leaf
1 cup half-and-half
sour cream for garnish

Soak top and bottom of a medium clay cooker in water for at least 15 minutes. Place butter, onion and leeks in cooker. Cover, place in a cold oven and set temperature to 450°. Cook for 15 to 20 minutes. Add pumpkin, chicken broth, salt, curry powder, nutmeg, white pepper, ginger and bay leaf. Cook for an additional 15 minutes. Remove from oven, remove bay leaf and puree mixture until smooth. Stir in half-and-half. Taste and adjust seasoning. Return to oven and cook until heated through. Garnish with a dollop of sour cream.

HAMBURGER VEGGIE SOUP

A quick, throw-together soup, this can be varied by using any combination of vegetables. The meat can also be varied by using ground turkey. It's especially good served with a dollop of sour cream.

1 lb. ground beef
1 cup chopped onions
1 cup diced potatoes
1 cup diced carrots
1 cup shredded cabbage
1 cup sliced celery
4 cups stewed tomatoes

5 cups water
1/2 cup uncooked rice
1/2 tsp. dried thyme
1/4 tsp. dried basil
2 bay leaves
4 tsp. salt, or to taste

Soak top and bottom of a large clay cooker in water for at least 15 minutes. In a skillet, brown hamburger and onion; remove to clay cooker with remaining ingredients. Cover, place in a cold oven and set temperature to 375°. Cook for 1 1/4 hours. Test vegetables for doneness and cook longer if necessary. Taste and adjust seasoning.

SIDE DISHES AND VEGETARIAN ENTRÉES

SQUASH AND APPLE BAKE

Perfect for a cool fall day when you want something sweet and satisfying! Crystallized ginger is available in the spice section of most stores.

2 acorn squash
4 Golden Delicious apples
½ cup water, or apple juice
1 tbs. finely chopped crystallized ginger
¼ cup brown sugar, firmly packed
salt and pepper

Soak top and bottom of a medium clay cooker in water for at least 15 minutes. Peel squash, remove seeds and cut into 1-inch chunks. Remove cores from apples and cut into 1-inch chunks, leaving skin on. Pour water into cooker, add squash and apple pieces and sprinkle with remaining ingredients. Cover and place in a cold oven. Set temperature to 400° and bake for 40 to 45 minutes. Test for doneness by piercing squash with a fork — it should be tender.

ORANGE BRAISED FENNEL

Fennel is a forgotten vegetable that is reminiscent of licorice. Orange juice complements this flavor and gives you a unique vegetable dish to serve.

2 fennel bulbs
1 cup orange juice
1 tbs. cornstarch
2 tbs. butter, melted
1/4 cup brown sugar, firmly packed, or more to taste
salt and pepper

Soak top and bottom of a small clay cooker in water for at least 15 minutes. Wash bulbs, cut into slices or cut finely into shreds. Mix orange juice with cornstarch; add butter and brown sugar. Pour orange juice mixture into clay cooker and add cut fennel. Sprinkle with salt and pepper. Cover and place cooker in a cold oven. Set temperature to 425° and bake for 45 minutes or until fennel is tender. Taste and adjust seasoning.

SWEET CLAY CORN

I tried clay-baking corn with and without the husk, and the husked corn won hands down. By adding a little sugar to the water and a seasoning of choice you get very tender, sweet corn.

4-6 ears corn
1/4 cup water
2 tbs. butter, melted
1 tbs. sugar
salt
herbs or seasoning of choice, optional (such as
  marjoram, rosemary or basil)

Soak top and bottom of a medium clay cooker in water for at least 15 minutes. Husk corn and place in cooker. Pour in water and butter. Sprinkle with sugar, salt and if desired, add a seasoning of choice. Cover and place in a cold oven. Set temperature to 425° and bake for 30 minutes.

BAKED SQUASH

This simple recipe my mother used for baking squash improves considerably with clay cooking because the moisture is retained.

2 acorn squash
1/4 cup butter, melted
1/2 cup brown sugar, firmly packed
4 pinches ground ginger, optional
salt and pepper

Soak top and bottom of a medium clay cooker in water for at least 15 minutes. Cut squash in half, discard seeds and set in bottom of cooker with cut side up. Drizzle butter over squash and sprinkle with brown sugar, ginger, salt and pepper. Cover, place in a cold oven and set temperature to 400°. Cook for 45 minutes to 1 hour, depending on size of squash. Flesh should be fork-tender.

ROASTED GARLIC

The latest thing in gourmet appetizers! Garlic is roasted until it is tender enough to squeeze out as a paste onto bread rounds or crackers. Use any herb of your choice in place of the rosemary. Usually the garlic is presented as a whole bulb surrounded by bread rounds with knives on the side for spreading.

2 large whole garlic bulbs
olive oil
salt and pepper
1 tsp. whole-leaf dried rosemary

Soak top and bottom of a small clay cooker in water for at least 15 minutes. Remove some of the outer papery covering (but not all) from garlic bulbs. Cut about ½ inch off top of whole bulbs so garlic is exposed and can be extracted easily. Liberally brush each entire bulb with oil, sprinkle with salt and pepper and place rosemary sprigs between cloves. Set bulbs cut side up in cooker, cover and place in a cold oven. Set temperature to 350° and bake for at least 1 hour or until garlic is easily squeezed out of cloves. If desired, remove the lid, brush more oil on the bulb and bake for an additional 15 minutes for a browner, richer-looking bulb.

EGGPLANT ANTIPASTI (CAPONATA)

Serve this Italian appetizer with bread rounds or crackers. If you wish to add a little touch of heat, stir in a few drops of Tabasco.

1 eggplant, peeled and cubed
salt
1/4 cup olive oil
1 medium zucchini, chopped
1 large onion, chopped
3 cloves garlic, minced
1/2 cup diced celery
1 carrot, chopped
1 green bell pepper, chopped
1 1/2 cups drained canned tomatoes

1/4 cup chopped fresh parsley
2 tbs. tomato paste
1 1/2 tsp. dried basil
1/4 cup red wine vinegar
2 tsp. sugar
1/4 cup sliced stuffed green olives
1/4 cup sliced black olives
2 tbs. capers
salt and pepper

Soak top and bottom of a medium clay cooker in water for 15 minutes. Sprinkle salt on eggplant cubes and place in a colander. Allow to drain for 30 minutes. In a skillet, heat oil and sauté eggplant and zucchini until lightly browned. Add onion, garlic, celery and carrot and cook for an additional 10 minutes. Add remaining ingredients and pour into clay cooker. Cover, place in a cold oven and set temperature to 375°. Cook for 1 1/4 hours. Taste and adjust seasoning. Serve hot or cold.

HARVEST POTATOES

You have a choice of using the squashes or potatoes alone or combining several varieties. This is an ideal dish for the cool seasons.

3 lb. sweet potatoes, yams, winter squash and/or potatoes
2 Golden Delicious apples
½ cup butter, melted
½ cup grated Parmesan cheese
salt and pepper

Soak top and bottom of a small clay cooker in water for 15 minutes. Thinly slice sweet potatoes (yams, squash and/or potatoes). Pare, core and thinly slice apples. Coat bottom of clay cooker with 1 tbs. butter. Place a layer of potatoes in bottom of cooker; drizzle with 1 tbs. butter and 1 tbs. Parmesan. Sprinkle with salt and pepper. Repeat this same technique alternating between apples and potatoes until all ingredients are used. Press down firmly to compress vegetables. Cover, place in a cold oven and set temperature to 475°. Bake for 45 minutes, uncover, reduce heat to 425° and bake for an additional 30 minutes. Potatoes should be brown and crisp on top and around the edges. Test for doneness by piercing with a fork. Remove from oven and allow to stand for 5 minutes before serving.

PARSNIP JULIENNE

Servings: 4-6

Parsnips are a forgotten vegetable with a natural sweetness. Be adventurous and try something different for dinner.

1½ lb. parsnips
4 tbs. butter
¼ cup brown sugar
½ cup chicken stock
2 tsp. chopped fresh parsley
¼ tsp. nutmeg
pepper

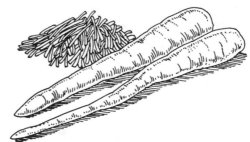

Soak top and bottom of a small clay cooker in water for 15 minutes. Peel parsnips and cut into thin matchstick strips. Place parsnips in clay cooker and cover with remaining ingredients. Cover, place in a cold oven and set temperature to 400°. Bake for 45 minutes to 1 hour, stirring once, until parsnips can be easily pierced with a fork.

POTATO CASSEROLE

This quick dish is easy to make and works great as a buffet dish.

9 medium potatoes, boiled until tender
1½ cups shredded cheddar cheese
1 can (10¾ oz.) cream of chicken soup
¼ cup butter, melted
2 cups sour cream
⅓ cup finely chopped green onions
1 cup crushed cornflakes or other crumbs

Soak top and bottom of a medium clay cooker in water for at least 15 minutes. Peel boiled potatoes and shred. In a bowl, mix cheese, chicken soup, butter, sour cream and green onions. Gently fold this mixture into shredded potatoes. Transfer to clay cooker and sprinkle with crushed crumbs. Cover, place in a cold oven and set temperature to 400°. Bake for 45 minutes. Remove lid and bake for an additional 15 minutes to brown the top.

STUFFED MUSHROOMS

Use as an appetizer or as a special vegetable presentation.

24 large mushrooms, stems cut off at base and reserved
½ cup butter, divided
½ cup minced onion
¼ cup minced shallots
½ cup cream sherry
¾ cup breadcrumbs

½ cup minced fresh parsley
½ tsp. dried tarragon
½ cup cream
salt and pepper
2 cups grated cheese (Swiss, Gruyère and/or Jarlsberg)
1 tsp. lemon juice

Soak top and bottom of a large clay cooker in water for at least 15 minutes. Finely chop mushroom stems and reserve for later. In a skillet, melt ½ of the butter and sauté onion and shallots until soft. Add chopped mushroom stems and cook for several minutes until excess moisture is cooked away. Add sherry, breadcrumbs, parsley, tarragon, cream, salt, pepper and 1 cup of the grated cheese. Stir gently to combine. Taste and adjust seasoning. Fill mushrooms, mounding in the center, and place in cooker. Sprinkle tops with remaining cheese. Place remaining butter and lemon juice in cooker. Cover, place in a cold oven and set temperature to 425°. Bake for 20 minutes or until mushrooms are tender. Serve warm.

BAKED ONION AND BROCCOLI

Servings: 4-6

Here's a creamy, delicious way to get kids to eat their vegetables. Cauliflower could be substituted for the broccoli but doesn't have quite the same eye appeal.

1 lb. fresh broccoli
3 medium onions
1/4 cup butter, divided
2 tbs. flour
1 cup milk
salt and white pepper

pinch nutmeg, optional
1 pkg. (3 oz.) cream cheese, softened
1/2 cup grated sharp cheddar or
  American cheese
1 cup soft breadcrumbs

Soak top and bottom of a medium clay cooker in water for at least 15 minutes. Cut broccoli florets into bite-sized pieces. Peel stems and cut into thin rounds. Peel onions and cut into small wedges. In a saucepan, melt 1/2 of the butter, stir in flour to make a roux and add milk, whisking until thickened. Add salt, white pepper and nutmeg to taste. Add cream cheese and stir until melted. Place broccoli and onion in cooker. Pour on sauce and sprinkle with grated cheese. Cover, place in a cold oven and set temperature to 425°. Bake for 25 to 30 minutes. Melt remaining butter and mix with breadcrumbs. Remove cover from cooker, sprinkle with buttered crumbs and bake until crumbs are browned, about 5 minutes.

MAPLE SYRUP BEANS

Most baked beans are made with brown sugar as the sweetener. This recipe uses maple syrup for a delightful change. Be sure to use the "pure" syrup for best results. It is important to discard soaking liquid because this will considerably reduce the gaseous effect of beans.

1 lb. dried navy beans
water to cover beans
1 medium onion, chopped
1/2-3/4 tsp. dried mustard
1/2 cup "pure" maple syrup
1/2 lb. salt pork, diced

Place beans in a bowl and cover with water. Allow to sit overnight. (If in a hurry, bring beans to a boil, cook for 5 minutes, remove from heat and allow to sit for 1 hour before using). Soak top and bottom of a large clay cooker in water for at least 15 minutes. Discard soaking water and pour on fresh water to cover. Add remaining ingredients and stir. Pour this mixture into clay cooker. Cover, place in a cold oven and set temperature to 375°. Bake for about 4 hours or until beans are tender, stirring occasionally.

PARMESAN POLENTA

Servings: 6-8

Polenta, a food common in Northern Italy, is a mush made of cornmeal which can be served as is or refrigerated, sliced and reheated. I like to serve it sliced with a drizzle of fresh tomato sauce running down the center. The word polenta refers to the finished product as well as to the coarsely ground cornmeal used to make it.

6 cups boiling water
2 cups polenta cornmeal
1 tsp. salt
1/4 cup butter
1/2 cup grated Parmesan cheese

Soak top and bottom of a medium clay cooker in water for at least 15 minutes. In a bowl, mix together the ingredients and pour into cooker. Make sure that mixture is at least 1 inch below edge of clay cooker to prevent spillage. Cover, place in a cold oven and set temperature to 375°. Bake for 45 minutes to 1 hour, stirring occasionally. Polenta should be thick, smooth and soft when done. If you desire a sliced polenta, pour mixture into a buttered loaf pan and chill until solid. Slice and reheat before serving.

TURNIPS AU GRATIN

Servings: 6

This creamy vegetable dish is an alternative to potatoes au gratin. For variation add a little grated Swiss cheese.

2 lb. turnips, peeled and thinly sliced
salt and pepper
½ tsp. dried thyme
¾ cup cream
3 tbs. butter

Soak top and bottom of a small clay cooker in water for at least 15 minutes. Place parchment paper in bottom of cooker and cover with a layer of turnips. Sprinkle with salt, pepper and thyme. Repeat until all turnip slices are used. Pour cream on top and dot with butter. Cover, place in a cold oven and set temperature to 400°. Bake for 1 hour or until turnips can easily be pierced with a knife. If you wish top to be browner, remove lid and bake for 5 to 10 minutes longer.

CARROT CUSTARD

Whole carrots line the bottom of this dish and a spicy carrot custard is baked on top.

4 large carrots, thinly sliced
3 cups shredded carrots
1/3 cup brown sugar
3 eggs, beaten
1/4 cup sour cream

2 tbs. grated orange peel
1 tsp. salt
1/4 tsp. cinnamon
1/4 tsp. ground ginger
1/4 tsp. ground cloves

Soak top and bottom of a small clay cooker in water for at least 15 minutes. Steam sliced and shredded carrots until tender (keeping them separated). Place parchment paper in bottom of clay cooker and place carrot slices along bottom and slightly up edges. In a food processor or blender, puree shredded carrots and remaining ingredients. Pour this mixture over sliced carrots. Cover, place in a cold oven and set temperature to 400°. Bake for 45 minutes or until custard sets.

CHEESY CORN BAKE

Instead of potatoes or rice, consider serving a creamy corn. This would be good served with a succulent roast and a green vegetable.

1 pkg. (18 oz.) frozen corn, thawed
⅔ cup evaporated milk
1 egg, beaten
2 tbs. chopped onion
½ tsp. salt
pepper
1 cup shredded Swiss cheese
1 tbs. butter, melted
½ cup soft breadcrumbs

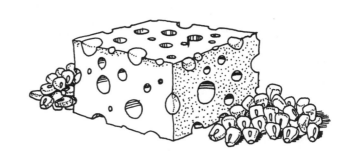

Soak top and bottom of a small clay cooker in water for at least 15 minutes. Place all ingredients in cooker except butter and breadcrumbs. Mix butter and breadcrumbs together and sprinkle on top. Cover, place in a cold oven and set temperature to 400°. Bake for 30 minutes. Remove lid and allow crumbs to brown for 5 to 10 minutes longer.

CHEESE SOUFFLÉ

Add a tossed salad and a fruit dessert to this vegetarian entrée.

4 tbs. butter
3 tbs. flour
1¼ cups half-and-half, heated
salt and pepper
1 tsp. Dijon mustard
½ tsp. dry mustard
¾ cup grated cheese (Swiss, Jarlsberg
   and/or Gruyère)

¼ cup grated Parmesan cheese
2 tbs. sour cream
2 tbs. sweet sherry
4 egg yolks
6 egg whites
¼ tsp. cream of tartar
¼ tsp. salt
grated Parmesan cheese

Soak top and bottom of a small clay cooker in water for at least 15 minutes. Melt butter in a saucepan, add flour and cook for 2 minutes. Add half-and-half, salt and pepper. Stir until mixture thickens. Remove from heat and beat in mustards, cheeses, sour cream, sherry and egg yolks. Set aside and allow to come to room temperature.

Beat egg whites until foamy, add cream of tartar and salt and continue to beat until stiff, but not dry. Fold ⅓ of egg whites into cheese mixture. Gently fold in remaining egg whites. Place parchment paper in bottom of clay cooker, pour in soufflé mixture and sprinkle with a little Parmesan cheese. Cover, place in a cold oven, set temperature to 450° and bake for 45 minutes or until top browns lightly. Serve immediately.

GREEK MILLET PIE

Millet is a neglected grain that is extremely good for you because it is a nonacid-forming grain. This recipe is a delicious vegetarian dish with an exotic flavor.

2 cups millet
4 cups vegetable broth
1 onion, finely chopped
1 cup ground pine nuts
½ cup chopped celery or green bell pepper
½ cup chopped fresh parsley
½ cup raisins
salt and pepper
4 tbs. butter
6 tbs. flour
2 cups milk
salt and white pepper
pinch nutmeg
1 jar (26 oz.) meatless spaghetti sauce

Soak top and bottom of a medium or large clay cooker in water while preparing ingredients. If time permits, soak millet in vegetable broth for several hours before cooking (but this step is not necessary). In a saucepan, bring millet and vegetable broth to a boil. Reduce heat and simmer for 15 minutes or until millet has absorbed all of the liquid. Stir in onion , pine nuts, celery (or peppers), parsley, raisins, salt and pepper. Remove from heat and set aside.

To make a white sauce, melt butter in a saucepan. Mix in flour, forming a paste. Whisk in milk and stir on medium heat until thickened. Add salt, white pepper and nutmeg to taste.

Place ½ of millet mixture in clay cooker, cover with spaghetti sauce and spread with remaining millet mixture. Top with white sauce. Cover and place in a cold oven. Set temperature to 475° and bake for 1 hour. Remove lid and bake for an additional 5 to 10 minutes to brown top of casserole. Allow to cool for about 15 minutes before serving.

VEGETARIAN LASAGNA

This recipe uses a bottled ragu, which saves a considerable amount of time.

1 lb. ricotta cheese
1 lb. grated Monterey Jack cheese
1 egg
1 tsp. dried oregano
1 tsp. dried basil
1/2 cup finely minced fresh parsley
2 tbs. vegetable oil

1 medium onion, chopped
1/2 lb. mushrooms, sliced
3 cups bottled meatless ragu sauce
1/4 tsp. anise seed
1 lb. dried lasagna noodles, boiled and
  drained
1/2 cup grated Parmesan cheese

Soak top and bottom of a medium or large clay cooker in water for at least 15 minutes. In a bowl, mix ricotta, Jack cheese (reserving 1 cup for sprinkling on top), egg, oregano, basil and parsley together. Heat oil in a skillet and sauté onion and mushrooms until wilted. Mix ragu with anise seed. Spoon a little ragu on bottom of cooker. Cover with a layer of noodles, a layer of ricotta cheese mixture, a little ragu, a layer of noodles and some mushroom-onion mixture. Repeat until all ingredients are used, ending with noodles. Sprinkle with reserved Jack cheese and Parmesan. Cover, place in a cold oven and set temperature to 400°. Bake for 1 hour. Remove lid to brown top for about 10 minutes. Allow lasagna to set for 10 minutes before cutting.

FISH AND SHELLFISH

DECORATED POACHED SALMON

Servings: 12

This will require a clay cooker large enough to hold a whole salmon, but the results are spectacular. A decorated salmon takes a little extra effort but I guarantee it will be the hit of the party.

COURT BOUILLON

¾ cup diced celery
½ cup diced carrots
½ cup diced onions
1 cup white wine

½ cup chopped fresh
  parsley
1 tsp. dried thyme
1 bay leaf
1 tbs. salt

8 whole peppercorns
2 qt. water (may vary due
  to size of cooker)
1 whole salmon, cleaned,
  about 5 lb.

Soak top and bottom of a large clay cooker in water for at least 15 minutes. Place all bouillon ingredients, except salmon, in clay cooker. (The amount of water added depends on the capacity of your cooker — water should be several inches below edge of clay cooker bottom.) Cover, place in a cold oven and set temperature to 450°. Cook for 40 minutes to develop flavor. Remove cooker from oven. Place salmon on parchment paper or cheesecloth (for easy removal) and set in bouillon. Make sure liquid is at least 1 inch below edge to avoid spillage. Cover, reset in oven and bake for 20 to 30 minutes or until salmon flakes easily. (Eye of salmon should be white.) Remove from oven, remove lid and allow salmon to cool in bouillon.

Carefully remove salmon from bouillon after it has cooled to room temperature. Place fish on a serving platter and with a sharp knife, carefully peel back skin and remove. Scrape any gray fatty material from meat.

GLAZE

1 cup mayonnaise	1 tsp. dried dill	1 tbs. unflavored gelatin
1 cup sour cream	1/2 tsp. Dijon mustard	1/3 cup cold water
1/2 tsp. salt		

Combine mayonnaise, sour cream, salt, dill and mustard together and set aside to bring to room temperature. Soak gelatin in water for 5 minutes, and then dissolve over medium heat in a small saucepan. Stir gelatin into dilled mayonnaise mixture and allow to cool. Spread glaze on fish, leaving head and tail unglazed.

GARNISHES (use any combination of the following)

green leaf lettuce	maraschino cherries	black or stuffed green olives
lemon slices or wedges	tomato slices or wedges	fresh parsley sprigs
cucumber slices		

Cut cucumber rounds into quarters and arrange cucumbers on fish, starting at the tail, overlapping them to resemble scales. Arrange other garnishes around the salmon. Cover the eye with an olive.

RED SNAPPER ADRIATIC

Servings: 6-8

Serve fish in a slightly more exotic way. If mussels are not to your liking, then substitute clams. Serve with a creamy risotto or potato casserole.

2 carrots, chopped
1 large tomato, seeded and chopped
1 small onion, diced
1 bay leaf
½ tsp. dried oregano
½ tsp. dried basil
1 cup dry white wine
½ cup clam juice
½ cup olive oil
¼ cup lemon juice
¼ cup minced fresh parsley
2 tsp. sugar
salt and pepper
1¾ lb. red snapper fillets
12 mussels
6-12 large prawns, tails left on, cooked or uncooked (see method)

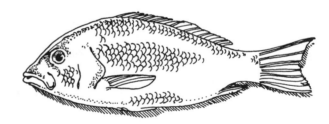

Soak top and bottom of a large clay cooker in water for at least 15 minutes. Combine all ingredients except seafood and transfer to clay cooker. Level of mixture should be at least 1 inch below edge of pot. Cover, place in a cold oven and set temperature to 425°. Bake for 30 minutes.

Remove from oven, slide snapper into sauce and arrange mussels around edge. Cover and bake for an additional 30 minutes. Remove lid. If any mussels are not open, take them out, wrap in foil and bake separately until opened.

If prawns are precooked, stir into hot mixture to warm. If uncooked, place in pot and bake for about 10 minutes or until prawns have turned pink. Remove cooker from oven. If sauce appears too runny, drain juices into a saucepan and reduce over high heat before serving. Place snapper in center of platter, pour sauce on top and artfully arrange mussels and prawns around edge.

DILLED SALMON

Serve hot with colorful stir-fried vegetables and parsley potatoes. This dish is also good served cold.

2 tbs. butter, melted
6 salmon fillets
1/4 cup red wine vinegar
1/2 tsp. dill weed
1/4 tsp. pepper

1/2 tsp. salt
1/2 cup cream
1/2 cup sour cream
fresh dill for garnish

Soak top and bottom of a medium clay cooker in water for at least 15 minutes. Place parchment paper in bottom of cooker and pour butter on top. Place fillets on top of buttered paper. In a saucepan, simmer vinegar, dill weed, pepper and salt together for 5 minutes. Mix together with cream and sour cream. Spoon mixture over salmon fillets. Cover, place in a cold oven and set temperature to 400°. Bake for 25 to 30 minutes or until fish flakes.

ITALIAN BAKED FISH

Parmesan and sour cream top a golden fillet. Consider serving with green bean salad in a subtle vinaigrette, a crusty bread and poached pears for dessert.

⅓ cup all-purpose flour
salt and pepper
2 lb. red snapper or sole fillets
2 tbs. butter
2 tbs. olive oil
1½ tbs. paprika

3 tbs. minced onion
½ cup grated Parmesan cheese
1½ cups sour cream
½ cup breadcrumbs
2 tbs. butter, melted
1 tbs. minced fresh parsley

Soak top and bottom of a medium clay cooker in water for at least 15 minutes. Blend flour, salt and pepper together and coat fish fillet. Melt butter and oil in a skillet and sauté fish fillets until brown. Cover bottom of cooker with parchment paper and place browned fillets on top. Sprinkle with paprika. Mix together onion, Parmesan and sour cream and spread on fish. Mix breadcrumbs with melted butter and parsley and sprinkle on top. Cover, place in a cold oven and set temperature to 400°. Bake for 30 to 40 minutes or until fish flakes easily.

CASHEW TUNA CASSEROLE

When you haven't done your shopping and need a quick dinner fix, this one is the answer. The cashews give this old standby a delightful difference.

2 cans tuna, drained
1 can (10¾ oz.) mushroom soup
1 cup finely diced celery
¼ cup minced onion
¼ cup water
salt and pepper
3 oz. crisp chow mein noodles
½ cup cashews

Soak top and bottom of a small clay cooker in water for at least 15 minutes. Mix all ingredients together, reserving a few noodles to sprinkle on top. Pour into clay cooker, cover, place in a cold oven and set temperature to 375°. Bake for 45 minutes.

SOLE VERA CRUZ

Sole is smothered in vegetables and of all things, stuffed olives. Serve with rice pilaf and creamy carrots.

2 lb. sole, cut into 6 pieces
1 tbs. lemon juice
¾ tsp. salt
¼ tsp. pepper
6 thin slices onion
1 tomato, peeled and chopped

½ cup diced green bell pepper
3 tbs. finely minced fresh parsley
2 tbs. olive oil
½ cup sliced stuffed green olives
1 tbs. flour mixed with 1 tbs. water,
  optional

Soak top and bottom of a medium clay cooker in water for at least 15 minutes. Place parchment paper in bottom of cooker. Place sole fillets on parchment paper; sprinkle with lemon juice, salt and pepper. Lay 1 onion slice on each fillet. In a bowl, mix together chopped tomato, green pepper, parsley, olive oil and green olives and spoon over fillets. Cover, place in a cold oven and set temperature to 400°. Bake for 25 minutes or until fish flakes. If you desire a thicker sauce, pour pot juices into a saucepan and stir in flour mixed with water. Stir until thickened and pour over fish on a platter.

STUFFED HALIBUT

Two halibut steaks sandwich a delicious vegetable and bread stuffing. To complete the meal, consider adding a colorful fruited jello salad and broccoli in a creamy cheese sauce.

2 halibut steaks, 1 lb. each
1½ tsp. salt
⅓ cup butter
1 cup grated carrots
¼ cup chopped celery
½ cup chopped onion
2 cups soft breadcrumbs
1 tbs. lemon juice
½ tsp. salt
¼ tsp. pepper
¼ tsp. dried thyme
2 tbs. butter, melted
1 tsp. lemon juice
paprika

Soak top and bottom of a medium clay cooker in water for at least 15 minutes. Place parchment paper in bottom of cooker. Sprinkle both pieces of fish on each side with 1½ tsp. salt. Place a fish steak on the parchment. In a skillet, melt ⅓ cup butter and sauté carrots, celery and onion until tender. Add breadcrumbs, lemon juice, salt, pepper and thyme and gently stir with a fork. Place stuffing on fish steak and cover with remaining fish steak. Combine 2 tbs. melted butter with 1 tsp. lemon juice, brush on top fish steak and sprinkle with paprika. Cover, place in a cold oven, set temperature to 425° and bake for 30 to 40 minutes or until fish flakes easily.

BAKED HALIBUT

To appreciate the subtle flavor of halibut, a simple bread stuffing rather than a highly spiced sauce is ideal.

2 tbs. olive oil
4 halibut steaks, about 1/3 lb. each
1/2 cup breadcrumbs
2 tbs. chopped fresh parsley
2 cloves garlic, minced
1/4 cup grated Parmesan cheese
salt and pepper
lemon slices for garnish

Soak top and bottom of a medium clay cooker in water for at least 15 minutes. Brush bottom of cooker with oil. Place halibut steaks in cooker. In a bowl, mix breadcrumbs, parsley, garlic and Parmesan; spoon mixture over steaks and sprinkle with salt and pepper. Cover, place in a cold oven and set temperature to 450°. Bake for 20 to 30 minutes (depending on thickness of steak). Garnish with lemon slices.

LINGUINI WITH RED CLAM SAUCE

Servings: 6

The trick with clams is not to overcook them. Clams tend to become rubbery when cooked too much, so always wait until the last moment before adding clams to most recipes.

2 tbs. olive oil
2 medium onions
2 cloves garlic, minced
1 tbs. chopped fresh parsley
4 cans (8 oz. each) tomato sauce
4 cans (7 oz. each) chopped clams
1 lb. linguini, cooked and drained

Soak top and bottom of a medium clay cooker in water for at least 15 minutes. Place oil, onions, garlic and parsley in cooker. Cover, place in a cold oven and set temperature to 425°. Bake for 20 minutes. Add tomato sauce and cook for an additional 40 minutes. Remove from oven, stir in clams and serve sauce over cooked linguini.

SEAFOOD LASAGNA

This is a creamy, delicious, somewhat exotic version of lasagna.

2 tbs. butter
1 cup chopped onion
16 oz. cream cheese, softened
1 cup cottage cheese
1 egg
2 tsp. dried basil
2 cans (10¾ oz. each) mushroom soup
⅓ cup white wine

½ cup milk
1½ lb. mixed cooked seafood (scallops, shrimp, salmon, crab and/or white fish)
1 pkg. (1 lb.) lasagna noodles, cooked and drained
1 cup shredded Monterey Jack cheese
½ cup grated Parmesan cheese

Soak top and bottom of a medium or large clay cooker in water for at least 15 minutes. In a skillet, heat butter and sauté onion until limp. In a bowl, blend cooked onion, cream cheese, cottage cheese, egg and basil. In a separate bowl, mix together mushroom soup, wine and milk. Gently fold in cooked seafood. Place parchment paper in bottom of clay cooker. Begin with a layer of cooked noodles, cover with a layer of cheese mixture, layer with noodles, and then layer with seafood mixture. Repeat until all ingredients are used. Top with shredded cheeses. Cover, place in a cold oven and set temperature to 400°. Bake for 45 minutes. Remove lid and bake for an additional 10 to 15 minutes to brown the top.

HOT CRAB BAKE

Servings: 8

This recipe is better if allowed to mellow overnight, but this step can be eliminated if you're in a hurry.

8 slices white bread, cut into ½-inch
  cubes
½ cup mayonnaise
1 green bell pepper, diced
1 medium onion, chopped
2 cups diced celery
2 cups crabmeat

4 eggs
3 cups milk
2 cans (10¾ oz. each) mushroom soup
1 cup grated Monterey Jack and/or
  cheddar cheese
paprika

Soak bottom of a medium clay cooker in water for at least 15 minutes. Sprinkle ½ of bread cubes in bottom of clay cooker. Mix mayonnaise, green pepper, onion, celery and crabmeat together and spread over bread cubes. Cover with remaining bread cubes. Beat eggs with milk and pour over entire mixture. Place in the refrigerator overnight. Soak lid of clay cooker in water for 15 minutes. Cover cooker, place in a cold oven and set temperature to 400°. Bake for 15 minutes. Remove from oven. Pour mushroom soup on top, sprinkle with cheese and top with paprika. Cover, return to oven and bake for 1 hour longer.

HOT SEAFOOD SALAD

This simple but elegant hot luncheon dish goes well with tender-crisp asparagus.

1 can (6 oz.) crabmeat
1 can (6 oz.) shrimp
1 cup mayonnaise
4 hard-cooked eggs, chopped
1 tsp. Worcestershire sauce
1 small onion, chopped
1 small green bell pepper, chopped
1½ cups fine breadcrumbs
¼ cup butter, melted

Soak top and bottom of a small clay cooker in water for at least 15 minutes. Mix together crabmeat, shrimp, mayonnaise, eggs, Worcestershire, onion and green pepper. In a separate bowl, mix breadcrumbs with butter. Dry inside of clay cooker with a towel. Sprinkle ½ of the buttered crumbs in bottom of cooker, cover with seafood mixture and sprinkle remaining crumbs on top. Cover, place in a cold oven and set temperature to 400°. Bake for 30 minutes. Remove cover for 10 minutes to brown top.

FAST JAMBALAYA

Here's a quick version of the time-consuming Southern favorite. If you like a little heat, add cayenne pepper or Tabasco Sauce to taste. Serve it with crusty bread.

4 thick slices smoked bacon, diced
1 medium onion, chopped
1/4 cup chopped green bell pepper
2 cloves garlic, minced
3 cups cooked rice

1 cup canned tomatoes
1 tsp. tomato paste
1 cup diced cooked chicken or ham
salt and pepper
6-12 precooked prawns

Soak top and bottom of a medium clay cooker in water for at least 15 minutes. Place bacon, onion, green pepper and garlic in cooker, cover and place in a cold oven. Set temperature to 450° and cook for 15 to 20 minutes or until bacon is browned. Remove from oven and add remaining ingredients except prawns. Return to oven, reduce temperature to 375° and cook for 20 to 30 minutes. Just before serving, stir in prawns to warm.

POULTRY

CORNISH HENS WITH SAFFRON RICE

Servings: 2-4

This is an easy one-dish meal that is absolutely luscious. Depending on your appetite, 2 hens can serve either 2 or 4 people.

2 Cornish game hens
pepper
Old Bay seasoning
1 cup uncooked long-grain rice
¾ cup chopped onion
½ cup frozen peas
½ cup chopped red bell pepper
½ cup sliced mushrooms

2 cloves garlic, minced
½ tsp. salt
¼ tsp. pepper
⅛ tsp. crushed saffron
1 can (14½ oz.) chicken broth
¼ cup white wine
½ cup grated Parmesan cheese,
  optional

Soak top and bottom of a medium clay cooker in water for at least 15 minutes. Sprinkle hens with pepper and Old Bay seasoning and set aside. Place remaining ingredients except Parmesan cheese in cooker and stir gently. Set hens on top of rice mixture and cover with lid. Place in a cold oven. Set oven to 425° and bake for 1¼ hours or until rice is tender. Taste and determine whether you wish to add Parmesan for a richer, creamier rice.

ROAST CHICKEN WITH ASSORTED STUFFING

Servings: 4-6

Clay cooking is ideal for roasting poultry. Use the technique described here but change the stuffing for variety. Stuffing recipes follow this page.

1 whole roasting chicken, about 4 lb.
2 tbs. vegetable oil, or melted butter
salt and pepper
2 tsp. dried herb of choice (rosemary, thyme, sage, etc.)
stuffing of choice (see pages 63, 64, 65 and 66)

Soak top and bottom of a medium clay cooker in water for at least 15 minutes. Rinse chicken and pat dry. Spread skin with oil or melted butter; sprinkle with salt, pepper and herb of choice. Make stuffing and fill neck and body cavities loosely. Wrap any remaining stuffing in aluminum foil and bake separately. Fold skin flap over stuffing and secure with poultry skewers. Place chicken, breast side up, in cooker. Cover and place in a cold oven. Set temperature to 475° and bake for 1¼ hours. Determine doneness by piercing thigh with a knife —juices should run clear, not pink. If you prefer a crispier skin, remove lid and allow chicken to brown for 5 to 10 minutes longer.

ITALIAN GROUND MEAT STUFFING

This creates a very hearty main dish that will really impress your company.

3 tbs. butter
1 small onion, minced
2 cloves garlic, minced
1 slice bread soaked in milk
$\frac{1}{4}$ lb. ground beef
$\frac{1}{2}$ lb. ground veal
$\frac{1}{4}$ cup grated Parmesan cheese
1 egg
1 tsp. dried rosemary
$\frac{1}{2}$ tsp. dried thyme
2 tbs. minced fresh parsley

Heat butter in a skillet and sauté onion and garlic until slightly wilted. Squeeze milk out of bread and discard. Add bread to onion mixture with remaining ingredients, mixing well. To determine if seasoning is correct for your personal taste, fry a small amount of stuffing and taste. Adjust seasoning if desired. Stuff loosely into poultry cavities.

CORNBREAD AND SAUSAGE STUFFING

Stuffs a 4 lb. bird

A Southern version of stuffing. If you prefer to use your own cornbread recipe, simply crumble about 1½-2 cups for this recipe.

½ pkg. (16 oz.) cornbread mix
6 oz. bulk pork sausage
¼ cup butter
1 small onion, chopped
½ cup chopped celery
¼ cup chopped fresh parsley

½ tsp. dried thyme
½ tsp. dried sage
½ tsp. poultry seasoning
½ tsp. salt
½ cup chicken broth
½ cup wine

Bake cornbread according to package instructions. In a skillet, brown sausage, transfer to a bowl and set aside. Pour off all but 1 tbs. fat. Add butter and sauté onion and celery until soft. Crumble baked cornbread into bowl with cooked sausage. Add onion, celery, parsley, thyme, sage, poultry seasoning and salt; mix well. Stir in chicken broth and wine until desired moisture is attained. Stuff loosely into poultry cavities.

HAM AND RAISIN STUFFING

This unique stuffing can be varied by using smoked ham or even cooked bacon in place of the standard ham.

1 cup dark or golden raisins
¼ cup sweet sherry, or orange juice
2 cups dry bread cubes
¼ cup butter, melted
½ cup chopped cooked ham
1 tbs. chopped fresh parsley
1 tsp. grated orange peel
salt and pepper

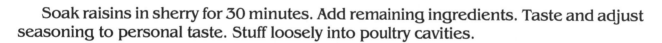

Soak raisins in sherry for 30 minutes. Add remaining ingredients. Taste and adjust seasoning to personal taste. Stuff loosely into poultry cavities.

MIXED RICE AND NUT STUFFING

Wild rice by itself is a little too strange for most people, so I mix it with white rice for a perfect balance.

¾ cup wild rice
¾ cup long-grain white rice
2½ cups chicken stock or water, divided
½ lb. bacon, diced
1 small onion, chopped

1 cup chopped celery
⅓ cup chopped fresh parsley
⅓ cup white wine
⅓ cup toasted pine nuts or almonds
salt and pepper

Cook wild rice and white rice separately in 1¼ cups stock or water until grains are just tender and set aside. In a skillet, fry bacon until fat is rendered and meat begins to brown. Remove bacon from skillet and sauté onion and celery in bacon fat until wilted. Using a fork, gently stir wilted onion-celery mixture and remaining ingredients into cooked rice. Taste and adjust seasoning. Stuff loosely into poultry cavities.

HONEYED CHICKEN WINGS

This is generally served as an appetizer but can also be used as an entrée. Add a little grated ginger root to vary the flavor.

3 lb. chicken wings
salt and pepper
1 cup honey
½ cup soy sauce
⅓ cup ketchup
2 tbs. vegetable oil
1-2 cloves garlic, minced

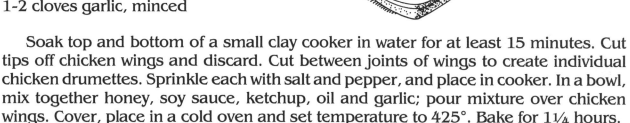

Soak top and bottom of a small clay cooker in water for at least 15 minutes. Cut tips off chicken wings and discard. Cut between joints of wings to create individual chicken drumettes. Sprinkle each with salt and pepper, and place in cooker. In a bowl, mix together honey, soy sauce, ketchup, oil and garlic; pour mixture over chicken wings. Cover, place in a cold oven and set temperature to 425°. Bake for 1¼ hours.

CHICKEN BREASTS WITH CHILE STRIPS

Servings: 6

This flavorful dish has a Mexican flare. Serve it with a salad tossed with a cumin vinaigrette and some cornbread or tortillas.

¼ cup butter, divided
¼ cup vegetable oil, divided
1 large onion, thinly sliced
18 canned peeled green chiles, cut into strips
6 small whole chicken breasts, boned and skinned
⅓ cup all-purpose flour
salt and pepper
⅔ cup milk or half-and-half
½ tsp. salt
2 cups sour cream
⅓ lb. grated cheddar and/or Muenster cheese

Soak top and bottom of a medium clay cooker in water for 15 minutes. Place ½ of the butter and oil in clay cooker with sliced onions and ½ of the green chiles. Cover, place in a cold oven and set temperature to 450°. Bake for 15 to 20 minutes or until onions are wilted and slightly brown. Meanwhile, cut each chicken breast into 4 fillets.

Mix flour with salt and pepper and dredge breasts in seasoned flour. In a skillet, heat remaining butter and oil and sauté chicken fillets until lightly browned. In a food processor or blender, puree remaining chiles with milk until smooth. Add salt and sour cream and stir until just mixed.

Remove onion and chile mixture from clay cooker. Place ½ of the chicken fillets in cooker, cover with ½ of the onion-chile mixture, ½ of the sauce and ½ of the cheese. Repeat with remaining ingredients. Cover, reduce oven temperature to 375° and bake for 30 minutes. Serve hot.

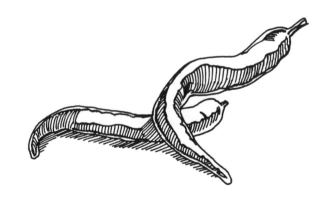

CREAMED CHICKEN ENCHILADAS

Servings: 4

Use poached shredded chicken in these enchiladas if you have it, but when you're in a hurry, canned chicken is a lifesaver. This is a "quick-fix" dinner that goes well with rice and a tossed salad with jicama added for crunch.

2 tbs. butter
1 medium onion, chopped
1 can (4 oz.) diced green chiles
1 can (14½ oz.) Mexican-style stewed
  tomatoes, drained
1 cup half-and-half

10 oz. medium cheddar cheese, grated
salt, pepper and cumin
8 thin corn tortillas
2-3 cans (12.5 oz. each) chunky white
  chicken meat
sour cream for garnish

Soak top and bottom of a medium clay cooker in water for at least 15 minutes. Heat butter in a skillet and sauté onions until soft. Add green chiles, tomatoes, half-and-half and cheddar cheese, reserving a small amount of cheese for topping. Stir until cheese melts. Add seasonings to taste. Dip tortillas in sauce, fill with chicken meat, roll and layer seam side down in clay cooker. Pour remaining sauce over top and sprinkle with reserved cheddar cheese. Cover cooker, place in a cold oven and set temperature to 400°. Bake for 40 minutes. For a darker top, uncover cooker and bake for an additional 5 to 10 minutes. Serve hot with a dollop of sour cream.

CHICKEN WITH TARRAGON

Servings: 4

Tarragon is reminiscent of anise or licorice flavor and perfectly complements this creamy chicken dish. Try it with a yellow rice pilaf and spiced green beans.

1 chicken, about 3 lb.
1 cup dry white wine
1 cup chicken stock
2 tsp. dried tarragon
salt and pepper
1 tsp. arrowroot
1 cup cream
fresh tarragon sprigs for garnish

Soak top and bottom of a medium clay cooker in water for at least 15 minutes. Cut chicken into 8 pieces. Place chicken skin side up in clay cooker. Mix together wine, chicken stock, tarragon, salt and pepper and pour over chicken. Cover, place in a cold oven and set temperature to 450°. Bake for 1 to 1¼ hours. Leave chicken in cooker, but pour liquid into a saucepan. Cover chicken with lid to keep warm while making sauce. Mix arrowroot with cream and stir into saucepan liquid, whisking over medium high heat until sauce has thickened. Place chicken on a platter and pour sauce on top. If available, garnish with fresh tarragon sprigs.

STUFFED CHICKEN SUPREME

Servings: 6

This recipe requires a little more effort but the results are worth it.

6 large chicken breast halves, boned and skinned
6 tbs. brandy

STUFFING

4 tbs. butter
2 tbs. minced shallots
1 tsp. minced garlic
½ lb. smoked ham, ground

½ tsp. dried thyme
2 tbs. chopped fresh parsley
½ cup grated Gruyère cheese
½ cup fresh breadcrumbs

SAUCE

1 cup dry white wine
½ cup chicken stock
2 tbs. butter
1 tsp. minced garlic
2 tbs. minced shallots
3 tbs. all-purpose flour

2 tsp. dried tarragon
½ cup cream
2 tbs. chopped mushrooms
2 tbs. chopped fresh parsley
salt and white pepper
2 tbs. grated Parmesan cheese

Soak top and bottom of a medium clay cooker in water for at least 15 minutes. Cut a pocket in each chicken breast half from thick side. Brush pockets with brandy. Make stuffing by heating butter in a skillet and sautéing shallots and garlic until wilted. Remove from heat and add remaining stuffing ingredients. Place stuffing in each pocket and pinch to seal. Place stuffed chicken breasts in clay cooker. Pour wine and chicken stock over chicken. Cover, place in a cold oven and set temperature to 450°. Bake for 1 hour.

In a saucepan, melt butter and sauté garlic and shallots until wilted. Add flour to garlic-shallot mixture and stir to make a roux. Remove cooker from oven and pour liquid into saucepan. Leave chicken covered in cooker to keep warm. Add remaining sauce ingredients to saucepan and stir until thickened. Taste and adjust seasoning. Place chicken on a platter and pour on sauce.

CHICKEN RICE CASSEROLE

Servings: 6-8

Cashews add a delicious texture balance to this easy casserole. Serve with a colorful fruit salad and a crunchy vegetable like broccoli.

1 cup uncooked rice
2 cups chicken broth
2 tbs. butter
2 cups diced celery
2 tbs. diced green bell pepper
¼ lb. mushrooms, sliced

1½ lb. canned chicken meat
½ jar (4 oz.) diced pimientos
1 can (10¾ oz.) mushroom soup
1 can (10¾ oz.) chicken rice soup
⅓ cup chopped cashews

Soak top and bottom of a medium clay cooker in water for at least 15 minutes. In a saucepan, cook rice in chicken broth until tender (about 15 minutes). In a skillet, melt butter and sauté celery, green pepper and mushrooms until slightly browned. Combine chicken, cooked rice, vegetables, pimientos and soups. Spoon mixture into cooker, cover, place in a cold oven and set temperature to 400°. Bake for 45 minutes, sprinkle cashews on top of casserole and bake for an additional 15 minutes without lid.

CHICKEN AND BROCCOLI BAKE

This quick dish is simply mixed all together and baked.

3 whole chicken breasts, cooked, cooled and diced
1/4 cup butter, melted
1/4 cup all-purpose flour
2 cups chicken broth
1/2 cup cream
3 tbs. cream sherry
1/2 tsp. salt
2 tbs. chopped pimiento
1/4 cup grated Parmesan cheese
2 bunches broccoli, coarsely chopped and steamed

Soak top and bottom of a medium clay cooker in water for at least 15 minutes. Place all ingredients in cooker. Cover, place in a cold oven and set temperature to 400°. Bake for 20 to 30 minutes.

BAKED RABBIT IN WINE

Servings: 4-6

If rabbit is not readily available, chicken can be substituted in this dish. Serve with mashed potatoes or rice, a crunchy salad and maybe a broiled stuffed tomato.

1 rabbit, 2½-3 lb.
salt and pepper
3 tbs. olive oil
2 tbs. butter
2-3 cloves garlic, minced
½ cup dry white wine
½ cup dry Marsala wine
1 tsp. ground dried rosemary
2 tbs. minced fresh parsley
pinch dried thyme
1 medium onion, chopped
¼ cup chicken broth
¾ lb. sliced mushrooms
1 tbs. cornstarch mixed with 2 tbs. water

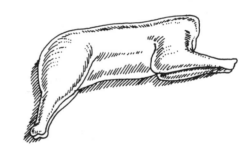

Soak top and bottom of a medium clay cooker in water for at least 15 minutes. Cut rabbit into pieces and sprinkle with salt and pepper. Heat oil and butter in a skillet and cook rabbit pieces until well browned. Mix remaining ingredients together except mushrooms and cornstarch. Place browned rabbit pieces in cooker and pour wine mixture on top. Cover, place in a cold oven and set temperature to 375°. Bake for 1¾ hours. Add mushrooms and bake for an additional 30 minutes. Remove rabbit and keep warm on a serving platter. Pour liquid into a saucepan and add cornstarch dissolved in water. Heat and stir until thickened. Taste and adjust seasoning. Pour sauce over rabbit and serve.

MEATS

GARLIC BEEF IN WINE

This simple casserole goes well with a good French bread and tossed salad.

½ cup red wine
1 tsp. Worcestershire sauce
1 tsp. dry mustard
3-4 cloves garlic, minced
dash Tabasco Sauce
4 lb. beef stew meat
salt and pepper
1 can (10¾ oz.) mushroom soup
1 cup crushed cornflakes or other crumbs

In a bowl, combine wine, Worcestershire sauce, mustard, garlic and Tabasco. Add beef and stir to coat. Place in the refrigerator and marinate for 3 to 4 hours. Soak top and bottom of a medium clay cooker in water for at least 15 minutes. Place marinated beef in cooker, sprinkle with salt and pepper and cover with mushroom soup, stirring to coat beef thoroughly. Sprinkle with crushed cornflakes and cover. Place in a cold oven, set temperature to 375° and bake for 2½ hours. Meat should be fork-tender. If not, continue baking for 15 to 30 minutes longer. Remove lid and allow top to crisp for about 10 minutes before removing from oven.

ROUND STEAK ROULADE

This easy-to-fix dish looks impressive, and tastes that way, too. Serve it surrounded by small onions and steamed red potatoes.

3 lb. round steak
salt and pepper
1 tbs. paprika
1/4 lb. mushrooms, sliced
1/2 cup sliced onion
1 jar (4 oz.) sliced pimientos, drained
2 cups breadcrumbs
1/2 cup butter, melted
1 egg
1/2 cup whole stuffed green olives, optional
flour seasoned with pepper for dredging
2 tbs. butter
2 tbs. olive oil
1 1/2 cups red wine
peeled small onions, optional

Soak top and bottom of a clay cooker in water for 15 minutes. Pound round steak until thin. Rub salt, pepper and paprika onto meat. Sprinkle with mushroom slices, onion slices and pimientos. Cover with breadcrumbs. Mix melted butter and egg together and drizzle over breadcrumbs. If desired, place olives in a row on the edge of the long side of steak. Starting with olive side, roll steak tightly and tie securely with baking string. Dredge meat roll in seasoned flour. Heat butter and oil in a skillet and brown meat on all sides. Place meat roll in clay cooker and pour wine around the sides. If desired, surround meat roll with peeled onions. Place in a cold oven and set temperature to 400°. Bake for 1½ hours.

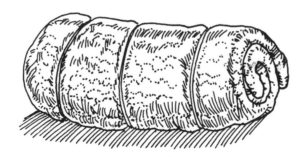

BEEF STEW

This recipe is slightly different than most stews because of the addition of apples and anchovy paste. Serve with noodles or cornbread and a tossed salad.

1½ lb. beef stew meat
½ cup all-purpose flour seasoned with salt and pepper
1 tbs. butter
1 tbs. vegetable oil
2 tart green apples, peeled and chopped
2 carrots, peeled and sliced
½ medium onion, chopped
1 can (14½ oz.) beef broth
½ cup dry red wine
½ tsp. anchovy paste
2 cloves garlic, minced
1 bay leaf
½ tsp. dried thyme
salt and pepper
1 tbs. cornstarch mixed with ¼ cup cold water, optional

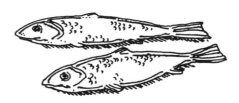

Soak top and bottom of a medium clay cooker in water for 15 minutes. Cut stew meat into 1-inch cubes and dredge in seasoned flour. Heat oil and butter in a skillet and quickly brown meat on all sides. Place meat in clay cooker. Add apples, carrots, onion, beef broth, wine, anchovy paste, garlic, bay leaf, thyme, salt and pepper; stir gently. Cover and place in a cold oven, set temperature to 450° and cook for 1¼ hours or until meat is very tender.

Remove from oven. If you desire a thicker sauce, pour liquid into a saucepan, mix cornstarch with ¼ cup water and add to sauce, stirring over medium heat until thickened. Pour mixture over meat and vegetables and stir. Taste and adjust seasonings.

NOTE: Sometimes meat tends to absorb much of the liquid, so if you desire a "saucier" stew, simply add some water to the saucepan before thickening with the cornstarch mixture.

STUFFED CABBAGE ROLLS

This is my father's favorite dish. It is a traditional dish served at special times in our family. It goes well with a good, hearty whole-grain bread.

1 large head green cabbage
¾ cup uncooked rice
½ cup chopped onion
¼ cup diced celery or green bell pepper
¼ cup diced carrots
1 lb. ground beef
1 tsp. salt
½ tsp. pepper
1 can (28 oz.) chopped tomatoes
½ cup vinegar
1 cup water or beef broth
½ cup sour cream, optional

Soak top and bottom of a large clay cooker in water for at least 15 minutes while preparing cabbage rolls. Steam head of cabbage for several minutes until cabbage softens, remove 6 to 9 large leaves and set aside. Shred ¾ cup of remaining cabbage and place in a bowl with rice, onion, celery (or green pepper), carrots, ground beef, salt and pepper. Mix thoroughly and form into balls about the size of a golf ball or tennis ball depending on the size of your leaf (and/or personal preference). Cut a V from base of steamed cabbage leaf and wrap leaf around meat, securing with a toothpick.

Place tomatoes, vinegar and water or beef broth in clay cooker and stir until mixed. Place cabbage rolls in liquid and cover with lid. (Make sure liquid is at least 1/2-inch below rim of bottom of clay cooker to prevent spillage during cooking). Place in a cold oven, set temperature to 400° and bake for 1 1/2 hours. Remove from oven and transfer cabbage rolls to a serving dish. Pour sauce over cabbage rolls or, if desired, stir sour cream into sauce and pour over cabbage rolls. Serve piping hot.

GERMAN SOUR MEAT (SAUERBRATEN)

This meat should be marinated for at least 24 hours or up to 3 days to get the characteristic sour taste. Clay cooking is ideal for this type of dish because the steaming creates extremely tender, succulent results.

5 lb. top round roast or rump roast
4 cups water
2 cups cider or red wine vinegar
1 large onion, sliced
1 tbs. whole juniper berries, optional
2 tbs. whole pickling spices
2 bay leaves
½ tsp. whole cloves
2 cloves garlic, peeled and crushed
2 tbs. sugar
2 tsp. salt, or to taste
1 tsp. black peppercorns
2 tbs. butter
3 tbs. all-purpose flour

Place meat in a large glass bowl. Add remaining ingredients except butter and flour. Allow to marinate for at least 24 hours or ideally up to 3 days, stirring occasionally. When ready to bake, soak top and bottom of a large clay cooker in water for at least 15 minutes. Heat butter in a skillet and brown meat on both sides. Transfer meat to clay cooker. Add flour to skillet, stirring to make a paste. Add marinade and cook for 3 minutes. Pour mixture over meat, cover and place in a cold oven. Set temperature to 425° and cook for 3 hours. Place meat on a platter. Strain gravy, taste and adjust seasonings, and pour over meat.

BEEF AND MUSHROOMS IN WINE

You'll love this French version of a wine stew. Serve with crusty bread, a tossed salad with a subtle dressing and a creamy potato or rice dish.

2½ lb. round steak
½ cup butter, divided
1 tbs. vegetable oil
10 oz. red wine
¼ cup all-purpose flour
2½ cups beef stock
2 bay leaves
2 sprigs fresh thyme
1 bunch fresh parsley
4 whole cloves
1 lb. mushrooms, sliced
3 cloves garlic, minced
salt and pepper
minced fresh parsley

Soak top and bottom of a large clay cooker in water for at least 15 minutes. Cut meat into 8 or 10 large pieces. Heat ½ of the butter and all of the oil in a skillet and brown meat well. Place meat in cooker. Add wine to skillet, bring to a boil and reduce to half the volume. Pour over meat. Melt remaining butter in skillet, stir in flour and cook until mixture becomes slightly browned. Add stock and whisk until mixture thickens. Pour stock mixture over meat. Enclose bay leaves, thyme, parsley stems and cloves in cheesecloth and wrap with a string. Submerge cheesecloth bag in sauce in cooker. Cover, place in a cold oven and set temperature to 375°. Bake for 1¼ hours. Add mushrooms, garlic, salt and pepper and continue to bake for an additional 45 minutes to 1 hour. Meat should be fork-tender. Remove cheesecloth bag and serve with a sprinkling of parsley.

TAMALE PIE

To save time, I used a skillet to brown the meats and vegetables. If you wish to use only the clay cooker, place the ingredients you wish to brown in the cooker, put the presoaked cooker in a cold oven, set the oven to 450° and allow 15 to 25 minutes of browning time.

1 lb. lean ground beef
1/4 lb. pork sausage
1/2 cup chopped celery
1/2 cup diced green chiles, or chopped
  green bell pepper
2 tbs. diced onion
2 1/2 cups pureed fresh or canned tomatoes
1 cup sliced ripe olives
1 tbs. chili powder
salt and pepper
1 can (16 oz.) whole kernel corn
1/2 cup yellow cornmeal
1 cup cold water
1 cup grated cheese (cheddar and/or Monterey Jack)

Soak top and bottom of a medium clay cooker in water for at least 15 minutes. In a large skillet, crumble beef and sausage and cook until browned. Add celery, green chiles (or green pepper) and onion and cook for 5 minutes. Stir in tomatoes, olives, chili powder, salt, pepper and corn. Mix cornmeal with cold water and stir into meat mixture until cornmeal thickens slightly. Taste and adjust seasonings. Pour mixture into clay cooker, cover and place in a cold oven. Set temperature to 375° and bake for 1 hour. Remove lid, sprinkle with cheese and continue to bake, uncovered, until cheese melts and browns slightly.

SWEET AND SOUR MEATBALLS

Serve this as a main course or an appetizer. If you serve it as a main course, it goes well with rice.

½ cup breadcrumbs
½ cup milk
1 lb. ground beef
¼ cup chopped onion
1½ tsp. salt
pepper
⅓ cup sliced green and/or red bell pepper

SAUCE

¼ cup sugar
1 tbs. cornstarch
1¼ cups water
¼ cup vinegar
1 tbs. soy sauce
½ tsp. salt

Soak top and bottom of a medium clay cooker in water for at least 15 minutes. In a bowl, combine breadcrumbs and milk and allow to stand for 5 minutes. Mix in ground beef, onion, salt and pepper. Form into 1-inch balls and place in cooker. Sprinkle sliced peppers around meatballs. In a separate bowl, combine sauce ingredients and pour over meatballs. Cover, place in a cold oven and set temperature to 450°. Bake for 1 hour and 10 minutes. Taste and adjust seasonings.

BEEF STROGANOFF

This quick and simple version of Stroganoff goes well with rice or noodles.

3 lb. lean beef
½ cup all-purpose flour
2 tsp. salt
½ tsp. pepper
2 tbs. olive oil
2 tbs. butter
1½ cups sliced onions
1 cup sliced mushrooms

2 cloves garlic, minced
2 cans (10¾ oz. each) mushroom soup
1½ tbs. Worcestershire sauce, or more
  to taste
1 tbs. Dijon mustard, or more to taste
salt and pepper
1½ cups sour cream

Soak top and bottom of a clay cooker in water for at least 15 minutes. Cut meat into strips 2 inches wide and ¼-inch thick. Combine flour, salt and pepper. Coat meat strips with flour mixture. Heat oil and butter in a skillet and quickly brown meat. Transfer browned meat to clay cooker, add onions, mushrooms, garlic, mushroom soup, Worcestershire, mustard, salt and pepper; stir to combine. Cover with lid. Place in a cold oven, set temperature to 350° and cook for 1 hour. Meat should be tender. If not, return to oven and cook for 15 to 30 minutes longer. Just before serving, stir in sour cream and return to oven until mixture is warm (but not boiling).

HAMBURGER GOULASH

Servings: 6

This entrée is simple to fix and tasty. The choice of noodles can vary the texture somewhat.

1½ lb. ground beef
1 large onion, chopped
salt and pepper
1 cup chopped celery
½ cup chopped black or stuffed green olives
1 cup grated American cheese
8 oz. dry pasta of choice, cooked and drained
1 can (28 oz.) chopped tomatoes

Soak top and bottom of a medium clay cooker in water for at least 15 minutes. In a skillet, brown hamburger and onion together and drain excess fat. Stir in salt, pepper and celery. Taste and adjust seasoning. Stir in olives and pour into clay cooker. Sprinkle with grated cheese and lay pasta on top. Spread canned tomatoes over pasta, including juice. Cover, place in a cold oven and set temperature to 400°. Bake for 30 minutes.

CORNED BEEF CASSEROLE

With kids you can't go wrong with meat, pasta and cheese. Serve with a tossed salad and a green vegetable.

1 can (12 oz.) corned beef
¼ lb. American cheese, shredded
1 can (10¾ oz.) cream of chicken soup
1 cup milk
½ cup chopped onion
1 pkg. (6 oz.) macaroni, cooked and drained
2 tbs. butter, melted
½ cup breadcrumbs

Soak top and bottom of a small clay cooker in water for at least 15 minutes. In a bowl, combine corned beef, cheese, chicken soup, milk and onion. Alternately layer corned beef mixture and pasta in clay cooker. Mix butter and breadcrumbs together and sprinkle on top. Cover, place in a cold oven and set temperature to 400°. Bake for 1 hour. Remove lid and allow top to brown for 10 minutes longer.

SPICED CORNED BEEF

Servings: 6

Vary the standard way of preparing a traditional Irish dish with this recipe.

3 lb. corned beef brisket
1 whole orange, sliced with peel
1 cup chopped celery
1 large onion, chopped
3 cloves garlic, crushed
1 tsp. dill seed
6 whole cloves
2 bay leaves
½ tsp. dried rosemary
4-inch stick cinnamon
water to cover beef

Soak top and bottom of a medium clay cooker in water for at least 15 minutes. Place all ingredients in cooker. Cover, place in a cold oven and set temperature to 450°. Bake for 1½ to 2 hours. Serve hot or chilled.

HAMBURGER HASH

Protein, starch and vegetables are all in one dish. You can make it spicier with the addition of some cayenne pepper.

1 lb. ground beef
3 medium onions, sliced
1 green bell pepper, chopped
1 can (16 oz.) chopped tomatoes
½ cup uncooked rice
2 tsp. salt
2 tsp. chili powder
¼ tsp. pepper
cayenne pepper, optional

Soak top and bottom of a small clay cooker in water for at least 15 minutes. In a skillet, brown ground beef with onions and green pepper; drain off fat. Add remaining ingredients and pour into clay cooker. Cover, place in a cold oven and set temperature to 400°. Bake for 1 hour. Taste and adjust seasoning.

SAGE MEAT LOAF

This is an extremely tasty meat loaf, with rather unusual ingredients.

2 lb. ground beef and sausage meat combined
2 eggs
1 cup oats
2 tsp. salt
¼ tsp. pepper
1 medium onion, chopped
1 cup applesauce
¾ tsp. dried sage
1-2 tbs. steak sauce

Soak top and bottom of a small clay cooker in water for at least 15 minutes. Mix all ingredients together except steak sauce. Form into a loaf and place in cooker. Brush top with steak sauce. Cover, place in a cold oven and set temperature to 450°. Bake for 1 hour or until loaf is well browned.

MEAT LOAF PIZZA-STYLE

Make meat loaf more interesting and tasty with this appealing recipe.

1 cup breadcrumbs or crushed crackers
1 cup milk
2 lb. ground beef
2 eggs, beaten
½ cup chopped onion
½ cup grated Parmesan cheese
1½ tsp. salt

pepper
1 tsp. dried oregano
1 can (8 oz.) pizza sauce
1 cup shredded mozzarella or Monterey
  Jack cheese
½ green bell pepper, chopped
1 cup sliced mushrooms

Soak top and bottom of a small clay cooker in water for at least 15 minutes. In a bowl, soak breadcrumbs (or crackers) in milk for 5 minutes. Add ground beef, eggs, onion, Parmesan, salt, pepper and oregano; mix well. Press into cooker. Cover, place in a cold oven and set temperature to 400°. Bake for 1 hour. Spread pizza sauce on top, sprinkle with cheese and top with green pepper and mushrooms. Cover, return to oven and bake for 10 minutes longer.

CHIPPED BEEF AND RICE CASSEROLE

Servings: 6

Instead of chipped beef, you can use other cooked meats such as ham, hamburger or even shrimp.

2 cups cooked rice
1½ cups chipped beef
½ green bell pepper, finely chopped
1 small onion, finely chopped
2 eggs, beaten
2 cups milk

2 cups grated sharp cheddar cheese
2 tbs. chopped fresh parsley
¾ tsp. dry mustard
1 cup fine breadcrumbs
2-3 tbs. butter, melted

Soak top and bottom of a small clay cooker in water for at least 15 minutes. In a bowl, mix rice, beef, green pepper, onion, eggs, milk, cheese, parsley and mustard. Pour rice mixture into clay cooker. Mix breadcrumbs with butter and sprinkle on top of rice mixture. Cover, place in a cold oven and set temperature to 375°. Bake for 45 minutes, remove cover and allow top to brown for an additional 10 minutes.

ITALIAN ROAST PORK

Roasts turn out absolutely succulent in clay cookers. This recipe has a stuffing of herbs and prosciutto ham which lends a subtle richness so the meat can be truly appreciated.

3 lb. boneless pork loin roast
3 cloves garlic, minced
1 tbs. olive oil
2 tsp. dried rosemary
10 fresh sage leaves (or 1½ tsp. dried)
salt and pepper
8 slices prosciutto ham
3 tbs. butter
3 tbs. olive oil
1 cup white wine
½ cup chicken broth
vegetables such as onions, carrots or potatoes, optional
1 tbs. cornstarch dissolved in 2 tbs. water, optional

Soak top and bottom of a large clay cooker in water for at least 15 minutes. Cut roast so that it is open and flat. Combine garlic with olive oil and spread on meat. Sprinkle with rosemary, sage, salt and pepper. Top with prosciutto slices. Roll roast tightly and secure with string. Heat butter and oil in a skillet and brown roast on all sides. Transfer roast to clay cooker. Add wine and broth to skillet and stir to scrape up browned bits. Add additional salt and pepper to taste. Pour sauce over roast. Cover, place cooker in a cold oven and set temperature to 425°. Bake for 1 hour and if desired, add roasting vegetables (onions, carrots, potatoes). Continue cooking for about 45 minutes or until internal temperature of meat registers 160°. Remove meat, cut strings and slice. If desired, thicken with cornstarch dissolved in water.

STUFFED PORK CHOPS

Keep in mind that this cooking technique can be used with any stuffing of choice. Pork is enhanced with an apple accompaniment such as applesauce, apple chutney or spiced apple rings. You will need a trussing needle and fine string for this recipe.

6 loin pork chops, ¾-inch thick
½ cup butter
2 stalks celery, finely chopped
1½ cups herb-seasoned stuffing mix
½ cup chopped toasted pecans
1 apple, peeled and finely chopped
salt and pepper
½ cup golden raisins
1 tsp. seasoned chicken stock base
apple juice
1 tbs. vegetable oil
1 tbs. butter

Soak top and bottom of a medium clay cooker in water for at least 15 minutes. Remove excess fat from chops and make a slit in one side of each chop for stuffing. In a skillet, melt ½ cup butter and sauté celery until limp. Add stuffing mix, pecans, apple, salt, pepper, raisins and chicken stock base. Stir to combine. Add enough apple juice to just moisten bread. Fill pork chop cavities with stuffing and sew opening closed with a trussing needle and string. In a skillet, heat oil and butter and brown chops on each side. Put browned chops in clay cooker, cover and place in a cold oven. Set oven to 425° and bake for 1 hour.

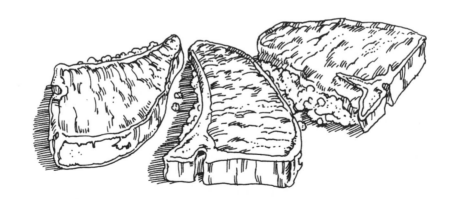

PORK CHOPS WITH SAUERKRAUT

This is an incredibly simple dish that has a slight sweet and sour quality. Consider serving it with mashed potatoes and a green vegetable.

2 lb. sauerkraut, drained
2 cups applesauce
2 tbs. brown sugar
¼ cup dry white wine
½ tbs. Dijon mustard
¼ tsp. pepper
6 pork chops, 1-inch thick
2 tbs. butter
2 tbs. vegetable oil

Soak top and bottom of a clay cooker in water for 15 minutes. In a bowl, mix together sauerkraut, applesauce, brown sugar, wine, mustard and pepper. Place mixture in cooker. In a skillet, brown pork chops in butter and oil. Transfer chops to top of sauerkraut mixture. Cover with lid and place in a cold oven. Set oven to 400° and bake for 1 hour or until chops are tender.

RICE AND PORK CASSEROLE

Servings: 4

This old-fashioned meal can be thrown together in minutes and forgotten until ready to serve. Goes well with lightly spiced poached apples.

1 cup uncooked rice
1 pkg. (1 oz.) onion soup mix
4 large pork loin chops
salt and pepper
1 can (10¾ oz.) mushroom soup
2½ cups water

Soak top and bottom of a small clay cooker in water for at least 15 minutes. Place rice in bottom of cooker and sprinkle with onion soup mix. Cut excess fat from loin chops, sprinkle lightly with salt and pepper and place on top of rice. Mix mushroom soup with water and pour over chops. Cover, place in a cold oven and set temperature to 400°. Bake for 1½ hours or until chops are tender.

BARBECUED RIBS

Precooking the ribs in a flavored poaching liquid helps to remove fat, flavor the meat and result in succulent, drop-off-the-bone tenderness.

3 lb. country-style ribs
water to cover
½ cup chopped onion
1 bay leaf

2 tbs. vinegar
1 tbs. salt
8 peppercorns

SAUCE

2 tbs. butter
1 medium onion, chopped
½ cup finely chopped celery
1½ cups ketchup
2 tbs. vinegar
3 tbs. Worcestershire sauce

1½ tsp. mustard
2 tbs. brown sugar
¼ cup lemon juice
½ cup water
salt

Soak top and bottom of a medium clay cooker in water for at least 15 minutes. Place ribs in cooker and cover with water. Add chopped onion, bay leaf, vinegar, salt and peppercorns. Cover, place in a cold oven and set temperature to 400°. Bake for 1¼ hours. While ribs are poaching, melt butter in a saucepan and sauté onion and celery until soft. Add remaining ingredients and simmer until thick. Remove clay cooker from oven, remove ribs and discard liquid. Replace ribs in cooker and pour sauce over them, coating well. Cover cooker, return to oven and bake for 45 minutes to 1 hour longer.

ISLAND SPARERIBS

This is an appetizer sparerib recipe that requires the butcher to cut the bones into bite-sized pieces. It is a delicious alternative to the standard chicken wings at a buffet party.

3½ lb. pork spareribs, cut horizontally
   into 1½-inch strips
½ cup sugar
½ tsp. salt
1 cup ketchup
1 tbs. hoisin sauce

1-2 garlic cloves, minced
⅓ cup brown sugar, firmly packed
1 tbs. honey
1 tbs. soy sauce
¼ tsp. ground ginger

Sprinkle ribs with sugar and salt and allow to stand for 1 hour. Soak top and bottom of a medium clay cooker in water for at least 15 minutes. Place ribs in clay cooker, cover and place in a cold oven. Set temperature to 400° and bake for 1¼ hours. While ribs are cooking, prepare sauce by mixing all remaining ingredients together. Brush sauce on ribs and bake for 15 more minutes. Turn ribs and brush with additional sauce, uncover and bake for 15 minutes longer. Serve hot.

BAKED SAUSAGE

The boring hot dog is replaced with a quick and delicious alternative.

2 lb. precooked sausage or wieners
1 can (20 oz.) crushed pineapple, drained
1½ cups brown sugar
2 tbs. Dijon mustard

Soak top and bottom of a medium clay cooker in water for at least 15 minutes. If you choose to use a large sausage like kielbasa, cut it into 1½-inch pieces and place in cooker. If using wieners, arrange them on bottom of cooker. Mix together crushed pineapple, brown sugar and mustard and pour over sausage or wieners. Cover, place in a cold oven and set temperature to 400°. Bake for 30 minutes.

LAMB STEW

This is a simple version of a Middle Eastern stew. Traditionally it is topped with chopped hard-boiled eggs, but this recipe calls for a sprinkling of parsley.

1/4 cup olive oil
1 large onion, chopped
2 1/2 lb. lamb, cut into 1-inch cubes
2 cloves garlic
1 bay leaf
2 whole cloves
2 1/2 tsp. salt

3 tbs. chopped fresh parsley
1/2 tsp. ground ginger
large pinch saffron
1 cup water, or more as needed
1 cup raisins soaked in water and
    drained, optional
1/3 cup toasted almonds, optional

Soak top and bottom of a medium clay cooker in water for at least 15 minutes. In a skillet, heat oil and sauté onion until golden. Place onion in clay cooker with remaining ingredients, except raisins and almonds. Cover, place in a cold oven and set temperature to 375°. Cook for 2 hours, adding more water if necessary. Taste and adjust seasonings. Meat should be fork-tender — if not, cook for an additional 15 to 30 minutes. If desired, stir in optional ingredients before serving.

QUICK BREADS AND YEAST BREADS

STRAWBERRY TEA BREAD

Serve this great tea bread at room temperature with honey butter as an accompaniment.

1½ cups all-purpose flour
1 cup sugar
½ tsp. baking powder
½ tsp. salt
1½ tsp. cinnamon

2 eggs
1 pkg. (10 oz.) frozen strawberries
⅔ cup butter, melted
⅔ cup chopped pecans

Soak top and bottom of a small clay cooker in water for at least 15 minutes. In a bowl, mix together flour, sugar, baking powder, salt and cinnamon. In a mixer, beat eggs well. Thaw strawberries, chop and add to eggs with juice from berries. Add dry mixture and melted butter and mix thoroughly. Fold in nuts. Place parchment or brown paper in bottom of cooker and pour mixture on top. Towel-dry lid, cover, place in a cold oven and set temperature to 375°. Bake for 1¼ hours or until a knife inserted in the center comes out clean. Cool for 10 minutes before removing from cooker.

APRICOT ZUCCHINI BREAD

Makes: 1 loaf

This moist, sweet bread is full of flavor. It's good served with apricot butter. Simply beat a little apricot jam into softened butter for a delicious spread.

½ cup vegetable oil
2 cups sugar
1 tsp. vanilla extract
2 eggs
1 cup grated zucchini
1 can (8 oz.) apricots, drained and chopped

1½ cups plus 2 tbs. all-purpose flour
1 tsp. baking soda
½ tsp. baking powder
½ tsp. salt
1 tsp. nutmeg
½ cup chopped walnuts

Soak top and bottom of a small clay cooker in water for at least 15 minutes. Beat oil, sugar and vanilla together with a mixer and add eggs one at a time, beating well after each addition. Add zucchini and apricots and beat well. Mix together flour, baking soda, baking powder, salt and nutmeg and stir gently into egg mixture. Stir in chopped nuts. Place parchment or brown paper in bottom of clay cooker and pour batter on top. Towel-dry lid, cover, place in a cold oven and set temperature to 400°. Bake for 1 to 1¼ hours or until a knife inserted in the center comes out clean.

ZUCCHINI NUT LOAF

Make this moist, dense, sweet bread with whole wheat flour if you wish. The flavor can be subtly changed by using lemon instead of orange extract.

2½ cups bread flour, or whole wheat flour
2 tsp. baking powder
1 tsp. baking soda
1 tbs. lemon peel
¾ tsp. salt
1 tsp. cinnamon
¼ tsp. ground ginger

2 eggs
1¼ cups sugar
½ cup vegetable oil
½ tsp. orange extract
2 cups shredded zucchini
1 cup chopped walnuts, optional

Soak top and bottom of a small clay cooker in water while preparing batter. In a mixing bowl, stir together flour, baking powder, baking soda, lemon peel, salt, cinnamon and ginger. Beat together eggs, sugar, oil and orange extract. Add flour mixture and stir until flour is incorporated. Stir in zucchini and nuts; mix well. Line bottom of clay cooker with parchment or brown paper and pour in zucchini mixture. Cover and place in a cold oven. Set temperature to 400° and bake for 1¼ hours or until a knife inserted in the center comes out clean. Remove from oven and allow to cool for 5 minutes. Run a knife around outside edge of loaf, remove from cooker and finish cooling on a rack.

CORNBREAD

This is a delicious, sweet cornbread that works very well in clay cookers. Great served with chili or stew.

¾ cup plus 2 tbs. sugar
½ cup vegetable oil
2 eggs, beaten
1½ cups all-purpose flour
1 tbs. baking powder
¼ tsp. salt
1½ cups cornmeal
1 cup milk

Soak top and bottom of a small clay cooker in water for at least 15 minutes. Blend sugar, oil and eggs together. Sift flour with baking powder and salt and add to sugar mixture with cornmeal. Stir in milk. Line bottom of cooker with parchment or brown paper and pour batter on top. Towel-dry inside of lid and place on cooker. Place in a cold oven and set temperature to 400°. Bake for 50 to 60 minutes or until top is slightly brown and a knife inserted in the center comes out clean.

PUMPKIN BREAD

Makes: 1 loaf

Sweet, spicy pumpkin bread reminds us of holiday times. For a change add pumpkin pie spice instead of cinnamon and nutmeg. Nuts can also be added.

1½ cups sugar
½ cup vegetable oil
2 eggs
¾ tsp. salt
¾ tsp. cinnamon

½ tsp. nutmeg
1¼ tsp. baking soda
1¾ cups all-purpose flour
1 cup canned pumpkin
⅓ cup water

Soak top and bottom of a small clay cooker in water for at least 15 minutes. With a mixer, beat sugar, oil and eggs together until mixed thoroughly. In a separate bowl, mix together salt, cinnamon, nutmeg, soda and flour. Beat flour mixture into egg mixture and add pumpkin and water. Cover bottom of clay cooker with parchment or brown paper. Pour in pumpkin mixture. Towel-dry inside of lid and set on top. Place in a cold oven and set temperature to 400°. Bake for 1 hour or until a knife inserted in the center comes out clean.

LEMON BREAD

Hot lemon syrup is poured on top of this delicious bread to make it even more moist and flavorful. It will crumble if you remove it from the cooker before it cools.

6 tbs. butter
1 cup sugar
2 eggs
1/2 cup milk
1 tbs. grated lemon peel
1 1/2 cups all-purpose flour

1 1/2 tsp. baking powder
1/4 tsp. salt
1 1/2 cups finely chopped nuts
juice of 2 lemons
2/3 cup sugar

Soak top and bottom of a small clay cooker in water for at least 15 minutes. With a mixer, cream butter and sugar together. Add eggs, beating well. Beat in milk and lemon peel. Combine flour, baking powder and salt and add to creamed mixture. Stir in chopped nuts. Wipe insides of both bottom and lid of clay cooker dry. Place a piece of parchment or brown paper in bottom of cooker and pour in batter. Cover, place in a cold oven and set temperature to 400°. Bake for 50 to 60 minutes or until a knife inserted in the center comes out clean. Make syrup about 10 minutes before bread is done. In a saucepan, heat lemon juice and sugar together until sugar dissolves. Remove loaf from oven, immediately pierce top of bread several times with a fork and pour lemon syrup over loaf. Allow to cool completely before removing from cooker.

DATE NUT BREAD

This very simple recipe makes a dense, moist, delicious loaf. Serve this bread with a pineapple cream cheese spread.

1 tbs. butter
1 cup boiling water
½ lb. chopped pitted dates
1 tsp. baking soda
1 cup sugar
1¾ cups all-purpose flour
1 tsp. vanilla extract
½ cup chopped walnuts or pecans

Soak top and bottom of a small clay cooker in water for at least 15 minutes. In a bowl, combine butter, boiling water and dates and allow mixture to cool to room temperature. When cooled, stir in soda, sugar, flour, vanilla and nuts. Line bottom of cooker with parchment or brown paper and pour mixture on top. Towel-dry lid, cover, place in a cold oven and set temperature to 375°. Bake for 1 hour or until a knife inserted in the center comes out clean.

PINEAPPLE CREAM CHEESE SPREAD

½ cup well-drained crushed pineapple
8 oz. cream cheese, softened
¼-½ cup powdered sugar, or to taste
chopped dates for garnish, optional

Beat all ingredients together until well incorporated. Serve in a bowl or ramekin with *Date Nut Bread*. If desired, sprinkle a few chopped dates on top.

WHOLE WHEAT BANANA BREAD

Makes: 1 loaf

This hearty, delicious bread is quick to fix and full of fiber. Whenever you have overripe bananas, simply peel them, place them in a bag and freeze until ready to use for baking.

½ cup butter, melted
1 cup sugar
2 eggs, slightly beaten
1 cup mashed bananas, about 3
1 cup all-purpose flour
1 cup whole wheat flour

½ tsp. salt
1 tsp. baking soda
⅓ cup hot water
1 tsp. banana extract
½ tsp. vanilla extract
½ cup chopped walnuts

Soak top and bottom of a small clay cooker in water for at least 15 minutes. With a mixer, cream butter and sugar together until smooth. Add eggs and mashed bananas, beating until smooth. In a separate bowl, mix together flours, salt and soda. Beat dry ingredients into butter mixture alternately with hot water. Stir in banana extract, vanilla extract and walnuts. Line bottom of clay cooker with parchment or brown paper. Pour in banana bread batter, dry inside of lid and set on cooker. Place in a cold oven, set temperature to 400° and bake for 1 to 1¼ hours or until a knife inserted in the center comes out clean.

SOUR CREAM BANANA BREAD

Makes: 1 loaf

There is a slight sour tang in this extremely moist bread. Chopped nuts can always be added as an option.

1 cup sugar
½ cup vegetable oil
2 eggs
½ cup sour cream (can use nonfat)
1 cup mashed ripe bananas
1 tsp. vanilla extract

1 tsp. banana extract, optional
1½ cups all-purpose flour
1 tsp. baking soda
1 tsp. baking powder
½ tsp. salt

Soak top and bottom of a small clay cooker in water for at least 15 minutes. With a mixer, beat together sugar and oil. Add eggs, sour cream, bananas, vanilla extract and banana extract, if desired, beating well. In a separate bowl, mix together flour, baking soda, baking powder and salt. Add dry ingredients to banana mixture, stirring until just mixed. Towel-dry inside of clay cooker and line bottom with parchment or brown paper. Pour mixture over paper and cover. Place in a cold oven, set temperature to 400° and bake for about 1 to 1¼ hours or until a knife inserted in the center comes out clean.

EGG BREAD (CHALLAH)

This is a delightful Jewish bread that is yellow, rich and slightly dense.

1½ tbs. yeast
1 cup warm water (not over 125°)
¼ cup sugar
1½ cups bread flour
2 tsp. salt
⅔ cup vegetable oil
¼ cup sugar
2 eggs
4 cups bread flour
1 beaten egg for glaze
poppy seeds or sesame seeds

In a bowl, dissolve yeast in warm water for 2 minutes. Add ¼ cup sugar and 1½ cups flour. Beat mixture with a wooden spoon until mixture resembles pancake batter. Cover with plastic wrap and allow to form a sponge for 30 minutes. Add salt, oil, sugar, eggs and flour, beating well. Knead mixture for 10 minutes. Divide dough into thirds, roll into cylinder shapes and braid (tucking ends under). Soak bottom of a clay cooker in warm water for 10 minutes and towel-dry inside. Line bottom of clay cooker with parchment paper or brown paper and place braided loaf on top of paper. Cover clay cooker with plastic wrap (not touching dough). Fill a sink with warm water. Carefully float clay cooker bottom (with dough) in water. Allow loaf to rise until double in bulk. Soak lid of clay cooker in water for at least 15 minutes. Carefully brush loaf with beaten egg and sprinkle with poppy or sesame seeds. Towel-dry inside of lid and place over risen loaf. Place cooker in a cold oven on the highest rack possible. Set temperature to 425° and bake for 45 minutes. Remove lid and allow to brown for several minutes before removing from oven.

COTTAGE CHEESE DILLY BREAD

A tasty, somewhat dense bread, this goes well with soup for a hearty meal.

1 tbs. yeast
¼ cup warm water
1 tbs. sugar
8 oz. large curd cottage cheese
1 egg
2 tsp. grated onion
2 tbs. butter, melted
2 tsp. salt
¼ tsp. baking soda
2 tsp. dill weed
1 cup whole wheat flour
1½ cups bread flour
1 beaten egg for glaze

Soak top and bottom of a medium clay cooker in warm water for 15 minutes. In a bowl, dissolve yeast in warm water. Stir in sugar, cottage cheese and egg, beating well. Add onion, butter, salt, baking soda and dill weed; mix well. Work flours in gradually and knead well for 6 to 8 minutes. Shape into a large, somewhat flat loaf. Towel-dry inside of clay cooker bottom. Line bottom with parchment or brown paper. Place bread on paper and float cooker bottom in warm water until dough is double in bulk. Before baking, cut ½-inch deep slits in wedge shapes around loaf and brush with beaten egg. Wipe out inside of lid, set on cooker and place in a cold oven. Set temperature to 425° and bake for 45 minutes. Remove lid and allow top to brown for about 5 minutes before removing from oven.

WHOLE WHEAT CINNAMON ROLLS

This makes hearty cinnamon rolls. For a "gooey" roll, use the alternative directions for sticky buns.

1 tbs. yeast
¾ cup warm water
¼ cup sugar
2 cups bread flour, divided
¼ cup butter

½ tsp. salt
1 egg
4 oz. plain yogurt
1 cup whole wheat flour

FILLING

½ cup butter, melted
1 cup white or brown sugar, firmly
  packed
2 tbs. cinnamon

1 cup raisins, soaked in hot water and
  drained
1 tbs. grated orange peel
1 cup chopped nuts, optional

In a bowl, dissolve yeast in warm water. Add 1 tbs. sugar and about 1 cup bread flour (or enough to make a thick paste). Using a wooden spoon, beat mixture for several minutes. Cover and allow to form a sponge in a warm place for 30 minutes. Add remaining sugar, bread flour, butter, salt, egg, yogurt and wheat flour. Knead for

6 to 8 minutes. If needed, add additional flour until dough can be just handled without sticking to your fingers. Soak top and bottom of a clay cooker in warm water while preparing dough. Roll dough into a rectangle about 10 x 12 inches. Brush dough with melted butter. Mix sugar and cinnamon together and sprinkle over dough. Sprinkle with raisins, orange peel and nuts (if desired). Roll up tightly from the long side. Cut into 1½-inch rolls. Wipe out inside of clay cooker bottom and line bottom and sides of cooker with parchment or brown paper. Place rolls in cooker, cover with plastic wrap and float in warm water until at least double in bulk. Wipe inside of clay lid and cover rolls. Place in a cold oven, set temperature to 400° and bake for about 45 to 55 minutes.

VARIATION: STICKY BUNS

½ cup honey

⅓ cup brown sugar

3 tbs. butter

¾ cup chopped nuts

Place honey, brown sugar and butter in a saucepan and heat slowly, stirring often. Pour mixture over parchment paper, sprinkle with nuts and place rolls on top. Bake as directed. As soon as you remove rolls from oven, turn over and remove parchment paper.

OATMEAL BREAD

Vary this simple, old-fashioned recipe slightly by your choice of sweetener.

1 tbs. yeast
1 cup warm water
1/4 cup honey, molasses or brown sugar
2 1/2 cups bread flour
2 tbs. dry milk powder

1 tsp. salt
2 tbs. butter, melted
3/4 cup oats
1 beaten egg for glaze
oats for topping

In a bowl, dissolve yeast in warm water. Add honey and about 1 cup flour. Stir with a wooden spoon into a thick paste, beating well for about 2 minutes. Cover with plastic wrap and allow to form a sponge in a warm place until double in bulk. Soak bottom of a small clay cooker in warm water for 15 minutes. While it soaks, add dry milk, salt, butter and oats to sponge mixture. Add remaining flour gradually, keeping dough soft. Knead well for 6 to 8 minutes. Wipe excess water from clay cooker bottom and line with parchment or brown paper. Shape bread dough into a loaf and place in cooker. Brush beaten egg over loaf and sprinkle with oats. Fill a sink with warm water and float cooker in water until dough is double in bulk. Soak cooker lid at the same time. Remove from water, dry inside of lid and set on top of risen bread. Place in a cold oven, set temperature to 425° and bake for about 45 minutes. Remove lid and allow top to brown for 5 to 10 minutes before removing from oven. Bread should sound hollow when thumped.

POTATO BREAD

A great way to use leftover potatoes! This dough can be used to make potato rolls, but reduce the baking time by 15 to 20 minutes.

1 medium potato, about 8 oz.
1 tsp. salt
½ cup water
1 egg
¼ cup butter, melted

¼ cup powdered milk
1 tbs. yeast
½ cup warm water
1 tbs. sugar
3-4 cups bread flour

Soak bottom of a small clay cooker in warm water for at least 15 minutes. Peel and dice potato. In a saucepan, add salt to water and boil potato until tender. Remove from heat and mash potato in cooking water. In a separate bowl, mix together egg, butter and powdered milk; stir in mashed potato. Dissolve yeast in warm water. Stir in sugar and potato mixture. Add enough flour to make a soft dough (that doesn't stick to your fingers), kneading for about 10 minutes. Wipe inside of cooker dry, shape dough and place in bottom of clay cooker. Float cooker in warm water until dough is double in bulk. Lid can be soaked at the same time. Dry inside lid and cover dough. Place cooker in a cold oven, set temperature to 425° and bake for 1 hour or until loaf sounds hollow when thumped.

GRUYÈRE HERB BREAD

Makes: 1 loaf

This delicious herb bread has cheese rolled into it. You'll need a large clay cooker in order to keep the ring shape.

1 tbs. olive oil
¾ tsp. dried basil
½ tsp. dried savory
½ tsp. dried chervil
½ tsp. dried tarragon
½ tsp. pepper
2 tbs. yeast
2 cups warm water
2 tbs. sugar
4-5 cups bread flour
1 tbs. salt
5 oz. Gruyère cheese, shredded

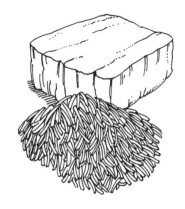

Combine oil, basil, savory, chervil, tarragon and pepper and allow to stand for 1 hour. Dissolve yeast in warm water. Add sugar and enough of the flour to make a thick paste. Beat for several minutes (mixture should be the consistency of pancake batter).

Cover and allow batter to rise in a warm place until double in bulk. Beat down; add herb mixture, salt and remaining flour. Knead for 6 to 8 minutes. Soak top and bottom of a large clay cooker in warm water while preparing dough. Roll dough into a circle and sprinkle with cheese. Bring edges of dough toward center, making a ball, and knead in cheese. Flatten dough into a 24-x-10-inch rectangle and roll into a cylinder, beginning on long side. Tightly pinch seam to seal. Dry inside of clay cooker bottom and place dough seam side down in a spiral or ring shape. Float base in warm water and allow bread to rise until double in bulk. Dry inside of lid, cover and place in a cold oven. Set temperature to 475° and bake for 20 minutes. Reduce temperature to 425° and bake for an additional 45 to 55 minutes or until bread sounds hollow when thumped. If you desire a darker loaf, remove lid and bake uncovered for 5 to 10 minutes before removing from oven.

BEER BREAD

This flavorful bread goes well with ham, cheese, steak and even shrimp. Be sure to use a dark beer for the best flavor.

1 cup dark beer
1 tbs. yeast
3 tbs. brown sugar
3-3½ cups bread flour, divided

1 tsp. salt
1 egg, well beaten
3 tbs. butter, softened
½ cup wheat germ

Heat beer to 115°, pour into a bowl with yeast and stir to dissolve. Add sugar and about 1½ cups flour and beat for several minutes until mixture resembles pancake batter. Cover with plastic and allow to form a sponge for 30 minutes. Add remaining ingredients and knead in just enough flour so dough does not stick to your fingers while kneading. Knead for 10 minutes. Form into a loaf shape. Soak top and bottom of a small clay cooker in warm water for 10 minutes. Remove bottom and dry inside with a towel. Place parchment paper in bottom of cooker and set formed loaf inside. Float clay cooker bottom in warm water until bread doubles in bulk. Dry inside of cover and set over bottom. Place in a cold oven, set temperature to 425° and bake until loaf sounds hollow when thumped, about 45 minutes.

HARVEST LOAF

A cluster of grapes decorates this large, hearty loaf of bread.

2 cups warm water
2 tbs. yeast
¼ cup brown sugar
2 cups bread flour

2 tsp. salt
1 cup oats
½ cup molasses
3-4 cups whole wheat flour

In a bowl, mix water and yeast together and allow to stand for 5 minutes. Add sugar and white flour and beat for several minutes. Cover and allow mixture to form a sponge for 30 minutes. Stir in salt, oats and molasses. Slowly stir in whole wheat flour. Knead until a stiff dough forms. Cover and allow to rise until double in bulk. Punch down and remove ¼ of the dough for grape decoration.

Soak bottom of a medium clay cooker in water for 10 minutes. Place parchment paper in bottom. Form a loaf and place in cooker. Form remaining dough into small balls and place in a triangle design on top of loaf. Use a little dough to shape a leaf and a few grape tendrils. Float bottom of cooker and lid in a sink filled with warm water until dough doubles in bulk. Dry inside of top, set over loaf and place in a cold oven. Set temperature to 400° and bake for 1 to 1¼ hours or until loaf sounds hollow when thumped. For a rustic effect, sift a little white flour over grape cluster.

DESSERTS

APPLE CRUMBLE

This dessert is a favorite any time of year. Don't limit yourself to only apples. Cut up any fruit of choice, use the same crumble topping and don't be afraid to experiment with alternative spices.

4 cups sliced apples
2 tbs. lemon juice
1/3 cup all-purpose flour
1 cup brown sugar, firmly packed
1 tsp. cinnamon

1/4 tsp. nutmeg
1/4 cup cold butter
1 cup oats
whipped cream or ice cream

Soak top and bottom of a small clay cooker in water for at least 15 minutes. Mix sliced apples with lemon juice and place in bottom of clay cooker. In a separate bowl, mix flour, brown sugar, cinnamon, nutmeg and butter together until crumbly, using a pastry blender or your hands. Stir in oats and sprinkle mixture over apples. Set cover on cooker and place in a cold oven. Set temperature to 450° and bake for 40 minutes. Remove cover and bake for an additional 5 to 8 minutes or until top is crisp. Serve warm with a small dollop of whipped cream or ice cream.

FRUIT CRISP

Pears and raspberries are very good, but the fruits can be varied to create delicious alternatives. This is a relatively low fat, low sugar dessert.

1½ cups pears or apples
2 cups raspberries, or berries of choice
⅓ cup dried currants or raisins
⅓ cup maple syrup, or more to taste
2 tbs. cornstarch
2 tbs. lemon juice
1 cup rolled oats

3 tbs. butter, melted
¼ cup honey
½ tsp. nutmeg
½ tsp. cinnamon
¼ tsp. ground cardamom

Soak bottom and top of a medium clay cooker for 15 minutes in water. Line bottom of cooker with parchment or brown paper. Peel, core and slice pears or apples and arrange in bottom of cooker. Sprinkle berries and currants (or raisins) on top. In a small bowl, mix together maple syrup, cornstarch and lemon juice; drizzle over fruit. Combine oats, butter, honey, nutmeg, cinnamon and cardamom together and crumble over fruits. Cover and place in a cold oven. Set temperature to 425° and bake for 35 minutes. Remove lid and bake for an additional 5 to 10 minutes or until top begins to crisp.

MEXICAN CHEESE DESSERT

If you're looking for something a little different, try this one. If you're feeling really adventurous, change the brandy to a flavored liqueur.

8 slices dry sponge cake
2 tbs. butter
1½ cups sugar
1½ cups water
¼ cup cognac or brandy of choice

4 eggs, separated
½ tsp. cinnamon
½ lb. Monterey Jack cheese, shredded
sweetened whipped cream for garnish

Soak top and bottom of a small clay cooker in water for at least 15 minutes. Cut cake slices into small squares. In a skillet, melt butter and fry cake until lightly browned; set aside. In a saucepan, bring sugar and water to a boil, reduce heat and simmer for 5 minutes. Remove from heat and add cognac. In a bowl, beat egg yolks until pale yellow in color. Add syrup in a slow stream, beating constantly. In a separate bowl, beat egg whites until stiff. Fold into egg yolk mixture with cinnamon. Cover bottom of cooker with parchment or brown paper. Place ½ of the cake squares on bottom, sprinkle with cheese and ½ of the egg mixture. Repeat with remaining ingredients. Cover and place in a cold oven. Set temperature to 400° and bake for 35 to 40 minutes or until custard is firm. Serve warm with a dollop of sweetened whipped cream.

AMARETTO PEACHES

Peaches go very well with almonds. This is a simple, light dessert that is ideal after a heavy meal.

6 ripe peaches
2 tbs. amaretto liqueur
1/3 cup ground blanched almonds
4 amaretto (Italian) cookies, ground
1 egg, separated
2 tbs. sugar

Soak top and bottom of a medium clay cooker in water for at least 15 minutes. Skin and pit peaches and scoop a small amount of pulp out of the center. Place peaches cut side up in bottom of clay cooker. Mix together pulp, amaretto, almonds, ground cookies and egg yolk. Beat egg white until stiff and add sugar. Fold into amaretto mixture. Place a small amount of filling in each peach hollow. Cover, place in a cold oven and set temperature to 400°. Bake for 35 to 45 minutes or until topping is firm. Serve hot or cold.

BLUEBERRY APPLE COBBLER

A cobbler is a satisfying, perfect dessert during the cooler seasons. For a little crunch, sprinkle a few toasted nuts on top of the whipped cream.

1 cup all-purpose flour
3/4 cup sugar
1 tsp. baking powder
1/2 tsp. salt
1 egg, beaten
2 cups fresh or frozen blueberries
2 cups sliced apples (prefer Granny Smith)

2 tbs. brown sugar
1/3 cup butter, melted
2 tbs. sugar
1/2 tsp. cinnamon
sweetened whipped cream or ice cream, optional

Soak top and bottom of a medium clay cooker in water for at least 15 minutes. Combine flour, 3/4 cup sugar, baking powder and salt and stir into beaten egg. Combine blueberries, apples and brown sugar together in clay cooker. Cover with batter and pour melted butter over all. Mix sugar and cinnamon together and sprinkle on top. Cover, place in a cold oven, set temperature to 425° and bake for about 40 minutes. Remove lid and bake for 5 to 10 minutes until top is browned. Serve warm, topped with a dollop of sweetened whipped cream or ice cream, if desired.

APPLE GINGERBREAD COBBLER

Apples perfectly complement this spicy cobbler and add a delicious moistness.

4 Golden Delicious apples, cored and sliced
½ cup sugar
1 tbs. lemon juice

BATTER

1 egg
¼ cup sugar
½ cup buttermilk
¼ cup molasses
1 cup all-purpose flour
1 tsp. baking soda
¾ tsp. baking powder
½ tsp. nutmeg
½ tsp. ground ginger
¼ tsp. cinnamon
½ tsp. salt
1½ tbs. butter, melted

Soak top and bottom of a medium clay cooker in water for at least 15 minutes. Mix apples, sugar and lemon juice together and place in cooker. Cover, place in a cold oven and set temperature to 400°. Bake for 30 minutes. Using a mixer, beat egg, sugar, buttermilk and molasses together. In a separate bowl, combine flour, soda, baking powder, nutmeg, ginger, cinnamon and salt. Beat dry ingredients into egg mixture. Add melted butter and beat well. Remove cooker from oven, pour batter over apples and bake for another 30 minutes or until gingerbread springs back when touched.

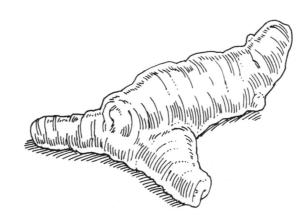

OLD-FASHIONED BREAD PUDDING

A family favorite. Toasting the bread gives the pudding a somewhat nutty flavor.

5 cups toasted bread cubes
5 cups scalded milk
1 cup raisins
4 eggs
1½ cups sugar
¼ cup butter, melted

½ tsp. cinnamon
⅛ tsp. nutmeg
1½ tsp. vanilla
pinch salt

Soak top and bottom of a medium clay cooker in water for at least 15 minutes. In a bowl, mix together bread cubes, scalded milk and raisins; set aside for 15 minutes. In a separate bowl, beat eggs, sugar, butter, cinnamon, nutmeg, vanilla and salt together. Pour mixture over bread cubes and gently stir together. Pour into clay cooker, cover and place in a cold oven. Set oven temperature to 400° and bake for 50 to 60 minutes or until custard is set.

DATE PUDDING

This rich pudding starts with a cake-like batter which is covered with a brown sugar syrup. Serve with a dollop of whipped cream.

1 cup chopped dates
1 cup milk
1 cup all-purpose flour
2 tsp. vanilla
1/8 tsp. salt
2 tsp. baking powder
1 cup brown sugar
1 qt. water
1/2 cup butter

Soak top and bottom of a medium clay cooker in water for at least 15 minutes. In a bowl, combine dates, milk, flour, vanilla, salt and baking powder; stir to combine. Place parchment paper in bottom of cooker and pour batter on top. In a saucepan, heat brown sugar, water and butter together and pour over batter. Cover, place in a cold oven and set temperature to 400°. Bake for 45 minutes.

MYSTERY PUDDING

Fruit cocktail is the mystery in this dessert. It is a simple dessert that can be served either warm or cool with a dollop of whipped cream or ice cream.

1¼ cups all-purpose flour
1 cup sugar
1 tsp. baking soda
¼ tsp. salt
1 egg, beaten
1 can (17 oz.) fruit cocktail, undrained
1 tsp. vanilla
½ cup brown sugar, firmly packed
½ cup chopped walnuts or pecans

Soak top and bottom of a small clay cooker in water for at least 15 minutes. In a bowl, combine flour, sugar, baking soda and salt. In a separate bowl, combine egg, fruit cocktail (including syrup) and vanilla. Stir wet ingredients with dry ingredients until just dampened (do not beat). Pour into clay cooker. Mix brown sugar and nuts together and sprinkle on top. Cover, place in a cold oven and set temperature to 400°. Bake for 40 to 45 minutes.

LEMON DESSERT SOUFFLÉ

A delicious light dessert is ideal after a heavy meal. This also makes a great dessert after an elegant dinner party.

2 tbs. butter
2 tbs. all-purpose flour
½ cup half-and-half
⅓ cup lemon juice
⅓ cup sugar

2 tbs. grated lemon peel
5 egg yolks
5 egg whites
⅛ tsp. cream of tartar
⅛ tsp. salt

Soak top and bottom of a small clay cooker in water for at least 15 minutes. In a saucepan, heat butter and stir in flour; cook for 2 minutes. Add half-and-half and whisk until thick. Remove pan from heat; beat in lemon juice, sugar, lemon peel and egg yolks. Cool to room temperature. With a mixer, beat egg whites until foamy, add cream of tartar and salt and continue to beat until whites are stiff but not dry. Gently fold egg whites into lemon mixture. Place parchment paper in bottom of cooker and pour soufflé mixture on top. Cover, place in a cold oven and set temperature to 450°. Bake for 45 minutes or until top browns slightly. Serve immediately.

CHOCOLATE SOUFFLÉ WITH CHOCOLATE SAUCE

Servings: 6

A delicious dessert is made even more decadent with a rich chocolate sauce.

6 oz. semisweet chocolate
1¼ cups cream
3 tbs. butter
4 tbs. all-purpose flour
1 tbs. vanilla
¼ cup rum
4 egg yolks
4 tbs. sugar
6 egg whites
pinch salt
2 tbs. sugar
powdered sugar for garnish, optional

Soak top and bottom of a small clay cooker in water for at least 15 minutes. In a saucepan, melt chocolate in cream over low heat. In another pan, melt butter, stir in flour and cook for 2 minutes. Remove pan from heat and add chocolate mixture. Stir in vanilla and rum. With a mixer, beat egg yolks with sugar until light and fluffy. Add chocolate mixture and allow mixture to cool to room temperature. With a mixer, beat egg whites with salt. Fold ¼ of egg whites into chocolate mixture to lighten. Gently fold in remaining egg whites. Dry inside of clay cooker and place parchment paper in bottom of cooker. Lightly butter sides of bottom and sprinkle with 1 tbs. of the sugar. Pour soufflé mixture into cooker, sprinkle with remaining 1 tbs. sugar, cover and place in a cold oven. Set temperature to 450° and bake for 30 minutes or until puffy and light browned on top. Serve immediately. If desired, dust with a little powdered sugar for garnish.

CHOCOLATE SAUCE

1 cup chocolate ice cream
½ cup cream, whipped
2 oz. dark crème de cacao liqueur

Allow ice cream to stand at room temperature for about 10 minutes. Fold in whipped cream and liqueur and serve with soufflé.

POACHED PEARS
WITH RASPBERRY SAUCE

This is taking poached pears to the ultimate. Instead of a banana split you have an elegant layered poached pear dessert.

4 large firm pears
3 cups white wine
1 cup water
1½ cups sugar
¼ cup lemon juice
1 tbs. grated lemon peel
dash cinnamon
¼ cup Grand Marnier liqueur, optional
10 oz. frozen raspberries, thawed
sugar to taste
1 qt. vanilla ice cream
1 cup cream, whipped
shaved chocolate for garnish

Soak top and bottom of a medium clay cooker in water for at least 15 minutes. Cut pears in half. Remove core with a melon baller. Trim stem and end off, but do not peel. In a saucepan, bring wine, water, sugar, lemon juice, lemon peel and cinnamon to a boil, stirring to dissolve sugar. Remove from heat. Stir in Grand Marnier (if desired). Place pears in cooker and pour syrup over pears. Cover, place in a cold oven and set temperature to 450°. Bake for 45 minutes or until pears are tender. Allow pears to cool in liquid. Place raspberries in a food processor or blender and puree until smooth. Add sugar to taste. Strain through a sieve to remove seeds. To serve, place a scoop of ice cream in a shallow dish and top with a pear half, rounded side up. Drizzle with raspberry sauce, top with a dollop of whipped cream and sprinkle with shaved chocolate.

APPLE COCONUT COFFEE CAKE

This tender cake can be served for breakfast or brunch. If you toast the coconut, you add a little more depth to the flavor.

¾ cup butter
1 cup sugar
3 eggs
1½ cups sifted all-purpose flour
2 tsp. baking powder
¼ tsp. salt

½ cup milk
1¼ cups flaked coconut
1½ cups sliced tart apples
⅓ cup sliced almonds
3 tbs. sugar

Soak top and bottom of a medium clay cooker in water for at least 15 minutes. Using a mixer, cream butter and sugar until smooth. Add eggs and beat well. Mix flour, baking powder and salt together and add to creamed mixture alternately with milk, blending until smooth. Fold in coconut and apples. Place parchment or brown paper in bottom of clay cooker. Pour in cake batter and sprinkle with almonds and 3 tbs. sugar. Cover, place in a cold oven and set temperature to 375°. Bake for 45 minutes to 1 hour or until cake springs back when touched.

DATE NUT MAYONNAISE CAKE

The dates and nuts can be eliminated in this recipe. For another alternative, try chopped, pitted prunes in the place of the dates.

2 cups sifted cake flour
1 cup sugar
¼ cup cocoa
2 tbs. baking soda
¼ tsp. salt
1 tsp. cinnamon
1 cup cold water

1 cup mayonnaise (don't use diet variety)
1 tsp. vanilla extract
1 cup chopped pitted dates
1 cup chopped walnuts

Soak top and bottom of a medium clay cooker in water for at least 15 minutes. Sift cake flour, sugar, cocoa, baking soda, salt and cinnamon into a bowl. In a separate bowl, blend water, mayonnaise and vanilla; fold into flour mixture. Fold in dates and nuts. Place parchment or brown paper in bottom of cooker and pour in batter. Cover, place in a cold oven and set temperature to 375°. Bake for 45 minutes to 1 hour or until cake springs back when lightly touched.

GERMAN BUTTERKUCHEN

This is a yeast cake with a sugar and almond topping. It is used sometimes as a breakfast or brunch coffee cake. If desired, serve with a dollop of whipped cream.

1 cup milk
½ cup sugar
1 tsp. salt
¼ cup butter
1½ tbs. yeast
1 tsp. sugar
¼ cup warm water
2 eggs
3¼ cups bread flour

TOPPING

½ cup butter, chilled
1 cup sugar
½ tsp. cinnamon
½ cup chopped almonds

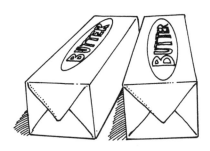

Soak top and bottom of a medium clay cooker in warm water for at least 15 minutes. In a saucepan, scald milk and add sugar, salt and butter. Stir to combine and cool to lukewarm. Dissolve yeast and sugar in warm water and stir into cooled milk mixture. In a large bowl, beat eggs with 1 cup of the flour. Add remaining flour alternately with milk mixture, mixing well after each addition. Dry inside of clay cooker bottom, line bottom and partially up the sides with parchment paper and pour in batter. Float in warm water until dough doubles in bulk. Using a pastry blender (or criss-crossing two knives), cut butter into sugar and cinnamon. Add almonds and sprinkle mixture over risen dough. Dry inside of clay cooker top and cover cooker. Place in a cold oven, set temperature to 425° and bake for 40 minutes or until cake is lightly browned. To serve, cut into squares.

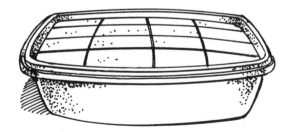

CHOCOLATE CHIP DATE CAKE

Servings: 8-10

Dates give this cake its rich moistness. Good served as an afternoon snack.

1½ cups boiling water
1 cup chopped dates
1 tsp. baking soda
½ cup butter
1 cup sugar
2 eggs, beaten
1½ cups all-purpose flour
¼ tsp. salt

¾ tsp. baking soda
½ tsp. baking powder
1 pkg. (12 oz.) semisweet chocolate
 chips
½ cup sugar
½ cup chopped walnuts

Soak top and bottom of a medium clay cooker in water for at least 15 minutes. In a bowl, pour boiling water over dates and 1 tsp. soda, set aside and allow to cool. In a separate bowl, cream butter and 1 cup sugar together. Add beaten eggs. Add cooled date mixture and beat until blended. Add flour, salt, soda and baking powder, beating well. Place parchment or brown paper in bottom of clay cooker. Pour batter into cooker. Mix together chocolate chips, sugar and chopped nuts and sprinkle over batter. Cover, place in a cold oven and set temperature to 350°. Bake for 1 hour and 10 minutes or until a knife inserted in the center comes out clean.

MIXED FRUIT LOAF

This loaf is somewhat reminiscent of a fruit cake with a subtle orange flavor. Great toasted!

2 tbs. butter, softened
1/2 cup sugar
1 beaten egg
3/4 cup milk
1/4 cup orange juice
2 tbs. grated orange peel

2 cups all-purpose flour
4 tsp. baking powder
1/2 tsp. salt
3/4 cup chopped walnuts
1/2 cup raisins
1/2 cup chopped candied cherries

Soak top and bottom of a small clay cooker in water for 15 minutes. In a mixing bowl, cream butter and sugar together. Beat in egg, milk, orange juice and orange peel. Mix flour, baking powder and salt together and beat into butter mixture. Stir in remaining ingredients. Dry inside of clay cooker bottom and place parchment or brown paper in bottom. Pour batter on top of paper. Cover, place in a cold oven and set temperature to 400°. Bake for 1 hour and 10 minutes or until a knife inserted in the center comes out clean.

OATMEAL CAKE WITH COCONUT TOPPING

This hearty cake is full of flavor with a delicious, moist topping.

1 cup quick oats
½ cup butter
1¼ cups boiling water
1½ cups cake or all-purpose flour
1 tsp. cinnamon
1 tsp. baking soda
½ tsp. salt
1 cup sugar
1 cup brown sugar, firmly packed
2 eggs, beaten
1 tsp. vanilla

Soak top and bottom of a medium clay cooker in water for at least 15 minutes. Place oats and butter in a bowl and pour boiling water on top. Stir until butter melts and set aside to cool. In a separate mixing bowl, combine flour, cinnamon, baking soda, salt, sugar, and brown sugar together. Beat in eggs, vanilla and cooled oat mixture. Dry inside of clay cooker, line bottom and up the sides with parchment or brown paper and pour in cake batter. Cover, place in a cold oven and set temperature to 400°. Bake for 45 minutes or until a knife inserted in the center comes out clean. Allow cake to cool completely and carefully remove from cooker. Place on an oven-proof serving platter, spread with coconut topping and place under a preheated broiler until mixture starts to bubble. Watch carefully. Serve warm or at room temperature.

COCONUT TOPPING

1 cup flaked coconut
1 cup chopped walnuts
2/3 cup brown sugar, firmly packed
1/4 cup cream
6 tbs. melted butter

Mix all ingredients together.

PASSION FRUIT CAKE

Passion fruit's unique flavor makes this cake unusual. Because this recipe uses a cake mix it goes together in minutes — just bake the cake and pour the glaze on top. The hard part is locating frozen passion fruit juice concentrate! You can use other frozen fruit juice concentrates as an alternative, or for variety.

1 pkg. (18¼ oz.) yellow cake mix
1 pkg. (3 oz.) lemon jello
1 tsp. vanilla
3 eggs
¾ cup water
¾ cup vegetable oil
1 can (6 oz.) frozen passion fruit juice
   concentrate
½ lb. powdered sugar
juice of 2 lemons
juice of 1 lime
¼ cup water

Soak top and bottom of a medium clay cooker in water for at least 15 minutes. With a mixer, beat together cake mix, dry jello mix, vanilla, eggs, water and oil until well mixed. Place parchment paper in bottom of cooker. Pour batter over paper. Cover, place in a cold oven and set temperature to 400°. Bake for 45 minutes. Cake should spring back to the touch when done. While cake is baking, make glaze. Thaw passion fruit concentrate and place in a saucepan with powdered sugar, lemon juice, lime juice and water. Stir over medium high heat until sugar is dissolved. Remove cake from oven, prick top all over with a fork and immediately pour on glaze. Allow cake to cool before serving.

APPLESAUCE CAKE

This spicy, moist cake can be varied by using dates instead of raisins or add candied fruits. I like this cake served warm with a dollop of whipped cream or a scoop of ice cream (or frozen yogurt).

½ cup butter
1 cup sugar
1 egg
1 cup applesauce
2 cups all-purpose flour
1 tsp. cinnamon

½ tsp. nutmeg
½ tsp. allspice
1 tsp. baking soda
2 tbs. hot water
1 cup raisins
½ cup chopped nuts, optional

Soak top and bottom of a medium clay cooker in water for at least 15 minutes. With a mixer, cream butter, sugar and egg together. Beat in applesauce. Mix flour, cinnamon, nutmeg and allspice together. Dissolve soda in hot water. Add flour mixture to butter-applesauce mixture alternately with soda water. Stir in raisins and nuts (if desired). Place parchment or brown paper in bottom of cooker. Pour batter on top. Cover, place in a cold oven and set temperature to 425°. Bake for 45 minutes or until cake springs back to the touch.

TOMATO SPICE CAKE

This moist, spicy cake has an unusual twist. Give it a try — you might be surprised.

½ cup butter
1 cup sugar
1 egg
1½ cups cake or all-purpose flour
1 tsp. baking soda
1 tsp. nutmeg

1 tsp. cinnamon
¾ tsp. cloves
1 can (10¾ oz.) undiluted tomato soup
1 cup chopped nuts
1 cup raisins

Soak top and bottom of a medium clay cooker in water for at least 15 minutes. With a mixer, cream butter, sugar and egg together. Mix flour, soda, nutmeg, cinnamon and cloves together. Add flour mixture alternately with tomato soup to butter mixture. Stir in nuts and raisins. Place parchment paper in bottom of cooker and pour in batter. Cover, place in a cold oven and set temperature to 425°. Bake for 45 minutes or until cake springs back to the touch.

CHOCOLATE RIPPLE CAKE

Servings: 8-10

Even if you rarely use cake mixes, this recipe will become a family favorite. It has a yummy cream cheese coconut filling.

1 pkg. (18¼ oz.) chocolate fudge cake mix
1 cup water
½ cup sour cream
4 eggs, divided
8 oz. cream cheese
⅓ cup sugar
1 cup flaked coconut

Soak top and bottom of a small clay cooker in water while preparing cake batter. With a mixer, beat cake mix, water, sour cream and 2 eggs together until well mixed; set aside. In a separate bowl, beat together 8 oz. cream cheese, sugar and remaining 2 eggs until creamy. Stir in coconut. Line bottom of clay cooker with parchment or brown paper. Pour in ½ of the chocolate mixture, spread cream cheese mixture on top and finish with remaining chocolate mixture. Cover and place in a cold oven. Set temperature to 400° and bake for 50 to 60 minutes or until a knife inserted in the center comes out clean. Cool completely before frosting.

FROSTING

1 pkg. fudge frosting mix
8 oz. cream cheese
⅓ cup lukewarm water

Blend frosting mix, cream cheese and water together until smooth. Add more water if frosting is too thick.

SOUR CREAM SPICE CAKE

Servings: 12

This is the type of cake my grandmother used to make — spicy, a tinge of molasses and loaded with raisins and nuts.

½ cup butter
1 cup sugar
½ cup molasses
2 eggs
2 cups cake flour
¾ cup raisins
¾ cup chopped nuts

1 tsp. cinnamon
1 tsp. nutmeg
1½ tsp. baking soda
¼ tsp. baking powder
¼ tsp. salt
1 cup sour cream

Soak top and bottom of a medium clay cooker in water for 15 minutes. With a mixer, cream butter and sugar together. Beat in molasses and eggs. Take a little of the cake flour and mix with raisins and nuts (the flour helps to keep raisins and nuts from sinking to the bottom of the batter). Mix together remaining flour, cinnamon, nutmeg, baking soda, baking powder and salt. Beat dry ingredients into butter mixture alternately with sour cream. Stir in raisins and nuts. Cover bottom of cooker with parchment or brown paper and pour in batter. Cover, place in a cold oven and set temperature to 400°. Bake for 50 to 60 minutes or until a knife inserted in the center comes out clean.

INDEX

Cake
  apple coconut coffee 152
  applesauce 162
  chocolate chip date 156
  chocolate ripple 164
  date nut mayonnaise 153
  German butterkuchen 154
  mixed fruit loaf 157
  oatmeal, with coconut
    topping 158
  passion fruit 160
  sour cream spice 166
  tomato spice 163
Caponata (eggplant antipasti)
  28
Carrot custard 37
Cheese soufflé 39
Cheesy corn bake 38
Chicken
  and broccoli bake 75
  breasts with chile strips 68
  enchiladas, creamed 70
  rice casserole 74

  roasted with assorted
    stuffing 62
  supreme, stuffed 72
  wings, honeyed 67
  with tarragon 71
Chipped beef and rice
  casserole 101
Chocolate
  chip date cake 156
  ripple cake 164
  soufflé with chocolate sauce
    148
Clay cookers
  care 4
  styles 5
Clay cooking
  advantages 1
  microwave 3
  rules 2
Cobbler
  apple gingerbread 142
  blueberry apple 141
Corn, sweet clay 25
Cornbread 117

Corned beef
  casserole 96
  spiced 97
Cornish hens with saffron rice 61
Cottage cheese dilly bread 126
Crab bake, hot 57
Croutons, garlic 15

Date
  nut bread 120
  nut mayonnaise cake 153
  pudding 145
Desserts
  amaretto peaches 140
  apple crumble 137
  apple gingerbread cobbler
    142
  blueberry apple cobbler 141
  chocolate soufflé with
    chocolate sauce 148
  date pudding 145
  fruit crisp 138
  lemon soufflé 147
  Mexican cheese 139

SERVE CREATIVE, EASY, NUTRITIOUS MEALS WITH NITTY GRITTY® COOKBOOKS

Extra-Special Crockery Pot Recipes
Cooking in Clay
Marinades
Deep Fried Indulgences
Cooking with Parchment Paper
The Garlic Cookbook
Flatbreads From Around the World
From Your Ice Cream Maker
Favorite Cookie Recipes
Cappuccino/Espresso: The Book of Beverages
Indoor Grilling
Slow Cooking
The Best Pizza is Made at Home
The Well Dressed Potato
Convection Oven Cookery
The Steamer Cookbook
The Pasta Machine Cookbook
The Versatile Rice Cooker

The Dehydrator Cookbook
The Bread Machine Cookbook
The Bread Machine Cookbook II
The Bread Machine Cookbook III
The Bread Machine Cookbook IV
The Bread Machine Cookbook V
Worldwide Sourdoughs From Your Bread Machine
Recipes for the Pressure Cooker
The New Blender Book
The Sandwich Maker Cookbook
Waffles
The Coffee Book
The Juicer Book
The Juicer Book II
Bread Baking (traditional), revised
No Salt, No Sugar, No Fat Cookbook

Cooking for 1 or 2
Quick and Easy Pasta Recipes
The 9x13 Pan Cookbook
Chocolate Cherry Tortes and Other Lowfat Delights
Low Fat American Favorites
Now That's Italian!
Fabulous Fiber Cookery
Low Salt, Low Sugar, Low Fat Desserts
Healthy Cooking on the Run
Healthy Snacks for Kids
Muffins, Nut Breads and More
The Wok
New Ways to Enjoy Chicken
Favorite Seafood Recipes
New International Fondue Cookbook

Write or call for our free catalog.
BRISTOL PUBLISHING ENTERPRISES, INC.
P.O. Box 1737, San Leandro, CA 94577
(800) 346-4889; in California (510) 895-4461